Rotterdam

Jon Brittain is an Olivier Award-winning playwright, comedy writer and director. His plays include *The Wake, The Sexual Awakening of Peter Mayo, What Would Spock Do?* and *A Super Happy Story (About Feeling Super Sad).* He co-created the critically acclaimed show *Margaret Thatcher Queen of Soho* and its sequel *Margaret Thatcher Queen of Game Shows.* He was one of the 503Five 2012/2013 and has worked extensively with Old Vic New Voices. He has written for Radio 4's *The Now Show* and Cartoon Network's *The Amazing World of Gumball,* and created and starred in the online sketch show *HodgePodge.* He directed both of John Kearns's Fosters Award winning stand-up shows *Sight Gags for Perverts* and *Shtick,* and Tom Allen's shows *Both Worlds* and *Indeed.* He was nominated for the Charles Wintour Award for Most Promising Playwright at the Evening Standard Awards in 2016 and *Rotterdam* won the Olivier Award for Outstanding Achievement in an Affiliate Theatre the following year.

Jon Brittain

Rotterdam

methuen | drama

LONDON · NEW YORK · OXFORD · NEW DELHI · SYDNEY

METHUEN DRAMA
Bloomsbury Publishing Plc
50 Bedford Square, London, WC1B 3DP, UK

BLOOMSBURY, METHUEN DRAMA and the Methuen Drama logo
are trademarks of Bloomsbury Publishing Plc

First published in Great Britain 2015

Reprinted 2017 (twice), 2018, 2019

image © Nick Rutter
graphic design © Rebecca Pitt

A catalogue record for this book is available from the British Library.

ISBN: PB: 978-1-3500-1833-4
ePub: 978-1-3500-1834-1
ePDF: 978-1-3500-1832-7

A catalog record for this book is available from the Library of Congress.

Series: Modern Plays

Typeset by Mark Heslington Ltd, Scarborough, North Yorkshire
Printed and bound in Great Britain

To find out more about our authors and books visit www.bloomsbury.com
and sign up for our newsletters.

Acknowledgements

It takes a lot of people to help me write a play and this one's been a particularly long time coming.

John Ginman was the first person I talked to about the idea for *Rotterdam* and luckily he was also the first to say that I should actually write it. I was supported every step of the way by my fantastic agents Lily Williams and Ben Hall and their assistants Jessica Coleman, Imogen Sarre and Charlie Weedon. I'm indebted to Leo Butler, Jude Christian and my friends from the Royal Court Young Writers' Programme for their feedback and advice. And I wouldn't have even finished the first draft without my friend and fellow playwright Lucinda Burnett, who agreed to read a new scene every day. On top of that, many others read drafts and gave feedback including (but not limited to) Tom Allen, Alex Brown, Melissa Bubnic, Gemma Langford, Brian Mullin, Evan Placey, Leonie Rae-Gasson and Tobi Wilson.

I'm really proud that the play is premiering at Theatre503, not only because they gave me the seed commission to write the first draft three years ago, but also because Paul Robinson, Steve Harper, Jeremy Woodhouse and the rest of their team have been unwaveringly supportive of me throughout my career and I am and shall remain incredibly grateful.

Once written, the play's biggest champion was Lisa Cagnacci, whose notes massively improved it and who also directed a reading at the New Diorama (a theatre that has also been very kind to me since programming my first play in 2010). Roy Williams made me feel like a much better writer than I am by selecting it for his *Playwright Presents* evening at Theatre503. And Suzi Ruffell, Alice White, Elisa King, Paul Heath, Rochenda Sandall, Keiran Hill, Lucy Phelps and Faye Marsay first brought the characters to life by taking part in readings and workshops.

In terms of research, there were numerous documentaries, books, TV shows and films that helped me get inside the characters' heads, but none were as useful as my discussions with Rebecca Root, Ash Palmisciano, Sally Higginson, Susie Gardener, and my friend Freddie Singleton, who read drafts, encouraged me and gave more than a few invaluable notes.

Last but not least, I want to thank Donnacadh, Alice, Anna, Ed, Jess, Richard, Keegan, Ellan, Jüri, Rob, Roxy, Ben, Ben, Mel, Anna, Daniel, Louis, Brian, Paul, Crystal and Tim for jumping on the ferry to Holland with me and making this happen, as well as Anna Brewer, John O'Donovan, Ellen Conlon, Neil Dowden and everyone at Methuen Drama for making *this* happen.

Beyond that there are a few people I'd like to thank just 'cause. Kenny Emson, Vinay Patel, David Byrne and all my other writer friends who stay up late on Facebook. Lucy Jackson, Ant Cule and Jack Swain, who were my theatre family for the first few years of my career. Tim Johanson, Mark Cartwright, James Seabright and the Thatcher team for keeping me in work. John Kearns and Matt Tedford, without whom I would have given up years ago. My granddad, who first taught me how to use my imagination. Isobel Condon and Carmel Winters, the teachers who encouraged me to write. Catie and Giles, with whom I spend most of my free time. Tristan Cass, who I miss very much. Mum, Dad, Kat, Justin, Bex, Tony, Karin and Liz, who I love. My brother Chris, who supported this play from the beginning and continues to teach me many lessons about how to be a better person. And Laura, who makes my life infinitely better just by being in it.

Right, so that's that. If you're reading this in the theatre please do remember to turn off your phones, if you're reading it in a bookshop please do think about buying it (I get a cut), and if you're me reading this in years to come I do hope you enjoyed the new *Star Wars* film as much as you hoped you would.[1]

Tot ziens,

Jon Brittain, October 2015

---

1 It was OK – *Jon Brittain, April 2017*

HARTSHORN-HOOK
PRODUCTIONS

Founded in 2007 by Louis Hartshorn and Brian Hook, H+H has produced over 70 shows, including *Woody Sez* (nominated for Best West End Musical, *Evening Standard* Awards), *Away From Home* (winner 24:7 awards Best Actor and MTA awards Best New Play) and *Some Small Love Story* (nominated MTM:UK award Best Lyrics).

Hartshorn – Hook has been an associate producer for the West End productions of *Urinetown* (Apollo Theatre) and *American Idiot* (Arts Theatre, UK Tour). Prior to producing the Olivier Award-winning *Rotterdam*, H+H took its *Rat Pack – Live* show to the Seychelles Islands, general managed the London transfer of Edinburgh Festival smash-hit *Kingmaker*, co-produced the Guild of Misrule's immersive production of *The Great Gatsby*, concluded the international tour of *Away From Home* with its final performances in Auckland, New Zealand, and produced a 400th anniversary production of *Richard II* in the Palace of Westminster.

Louis and Brian believe that *Rotterdam* is a rare gem of a play; it is touching, funny, powerful and true-to-life. They are honoured and delighted to have worked on the show.

THEATRE 503

Theatre503 is the award-winning home of groundbreaking plays

Led by Artistic Director Lisa Spirling, Theatre503 is a flagship new writing venue committed to producing bold, brave new plays. We are the smallest theatre in the world to win an Olivier Award and we offer more opportunities to new writers than any other theatre in the UK.

Theatre503 Team:
Artistic Director Lisa Spirling
Executive Director Andrew Shepherd
Producer Jessica Campbell
Literary Manager Steve Harper
Literary Coordinators Lauretta Barrow, Wayne Brown
Operations Manager Anna De Freitas
Resident Assistant Producers Michelle McKay, Laura Sedgwick
Senior Readers Kate Brower, Rob Young

Theatre503 Board:
Royce Bell, Peter Benson, Chris Campbell, Kay Ellen Consolver, Ben Hall, Dennis Kelly, Eleanor Lloyd, Marcus Markou, Geraldine Sharpe-Newton, Jack Tilbury, Erica Whyman (Chair), Roy Williams.

Theatre503 Heroes:
These brilliant volunteers give their valuable time and expertise to Theatre503 as front of house and box office managers, script readers and much more.

Alice Mason, Anna Middlemass, Anna Mors, Anna Landi, Andrei Vornicu, Asha Osborne, Annabel Pemberton, Bethany Doherty, Brett Westwell, Carla Grauls, Carla Kingham, Cecilia Garcia, Cecily King, Chelsey Gillard, Charlotte Mulliner, Chidi Chukwu, Damian Robertson, Danielle Wilson, David Benedictus, Dominic Jones, Elena Valentine, Emma Brand, Fabienne Gould, George Linfield, Gillian Greer, Imogen Robertson, Isla Coulter, James Hansen, Jim Mannering, Joanna Lallay,

Support Theatre503
Help us take risks on new writers and produce the plays other theatres can't, or won't. Together we can discover the writers of tomorrow and make some of the most exciting theatre in the country. With memberships ranging from £23 to £1003 there is a chance to get involved no matter what your budget, to help us remain 'arguably the most important theatre in Britain today'. (*Guardian*)

Benefits range from priority notice of our work and news, access to sold-out shows, ticket deals, and opportunities to attend parties and peek into rehearsals. Visit theatre503.com or call 020 7978 7040 for more details.

Volunteer With Us:
There are many ways to get involved in Theatre503, from joining our reading team to assisting during technical weeks or working front of house. If you're interested in volunteering please email volunteer@theatre503.com

Theatre503, 503 Battersea Park Rd, London SW11 3BW
020 7978 7040 | www.theatre503.com

@theatre503 | facebook.com/theatre503

Rotterdam

For Laura

Rotterdam was originally a seed commission for Theatre503's 503Five New Writing Scheme 2012. It received rehearsed readings at the New Diorama Theatre in 2014 as part of the *Brain of Brittain* season and at Theatre503 in 2015 as the Roy Williams edition of *Playwright Presents*.

Rotterdam received its world premiere at Theatre503, London, on 27 October 2015, in a co-production with Hartshorn – Hook Productions, before transferring to Trafalgar Studios, London, on 26 July 2016.

Alice	Alice McCarthy
Fiona/Adrian	Anna Martine Freeman
Lelani	Jessica Clark
Josh	Ed Eales-White

Director	Donnacadh O'Briain
Designer	Ellan Parry
Lighting Designer	Richard Williamson
Composer/Sound Designer	Keegan Curran
Movement Director	Jüri Nael
Fight Director	Rob Leonard
Associate Director	Roxy Cook
Assistant Designer	Anna Driftmier*
Assistant Lighting Designer	Daniel English
Company Stage Manager	Harriet Stewart**
Stage Manager	Benedict Hudson
Assistant Stage Manager	Melissa Berry*
Production Manager	Ben O'Grady*
	Nick Slater**
Producers	Louis Hartshorn
	Brian Hook
Associate Producers	Paul Virides
	Crystal Noll
General Manager	Heather Young
With Thanks	Gendered Intelligence
	Trans Media Watch

*Theatre503
**Trafalgar Studios

Rotterdam received its US premiere at 59E59 Theaters, New York, on 17 May 2017 before transferring to the Arts Theatre, London, on 21 June 2017, produced by Hartshorn – Hook Productions.

Alice	Alice McCarthy
Fiona/Adrian	Anna Martine Freeman
Lelani	Ellie Morris
Josh	Ed Eales-White

Director	Donnacadh O'Briain
Designer	Ellan Parry
Lighting Designer	Richard Williamson
Composer/Sound Designer	Keegan Curran
Movement Director	Jüri Nael
Fight Director	Rob Leonard
Associate Director	Roxy Cook
Assistant Lighting Designer	Daniel English
Stage Manager	Katie Jackson
Production Manager	Richard Williamson
Producers	Louis Hartshorn
	Brian Hook
Assistant Producer	Rebecca Morgan
Line Producer	Lucy Jackson
Assistant Line Producer	Brittany Coyne
General Manager	Heather Young
With Thanks	Gendered Intelligence
	Trans Media Watch
	Crystal Noll

Characters

Alice, *late twenties, female, British*

Fiona/Adrian, *late twenties, transgender male,* British*

Lelani, *twenty-one, female, Dutch*

Josh, *late twenties/early thirties, male, British*

** The character of **Adrian** is living as female at the beginning of the play and transitions to male during it.*

Notes

An ellipsis (. . .) indicates a speech trailing off.

A dash (–) indicates someone's speech has been interrupted, sometimes by themselves.

The play is set in various locations in and around the Dutch city of Rotterdam. Costumes and personal props should be represented realistically, but the rest of the set need not be.

This playscript was correct at the time of publication but may have changed during rehearsal.

Act One: Oud en Nieuw

Scene One

Alice *and* **Fiona**'s *flat.*

Dutch pop music plays.

Alice *deliberates over something she is writing on her laptop while* **Fiona** *watches her.*

The music finishes and **Alice** *puts down the laptop.*

Alice   Right. There. I'm finished.

Fiona   You're finished?

Alice   I'm finished, I'm done, I mean, I think I am, I think it's done.

Fiona   Do you want me to have a read?

Alice   No. No, it's fine. Unless . . . do you want to?

Fiona   If you want me to.

Alice   Right, yeah, no, no, you probably should.

Fiona   OK, I will.

Alice   Actually can you not?

Fiona   No?

Alice   No, and it's not that I don't want you to, I do, obviously, it's just I knew you'll find loads wrong with it and then you'll make me change it and –

Fiona   I won't make you change it –

Alice   And then I'll start worrying about all the other things that are wrong with it –

Fiona   I won't make you change it.

Alice   And then I'll never actually send it and we'll be right back where we started –

Fiona   Alice, I won't make you change it.

Alice   Yes, you would! You always make me change things.

Fiona   Like when?

Alice   Last week, last week I left that work in the kitchen –

Fiona   I made a few notes in the margin, I was just trying to make it sound less dry.

Alice   It was a shipping contract, it was supposed to sound dry. Look, I'd rather just send it, OK?

Fiona   Good, I want you to just send it.

Alice   Fine, I will.

Beat.

OK, alright, maybe you should take a look.

Fiona   Fine.

Alice   Actually no.

Fiona   *Seriously*?!

Alice   I'm sorry, I'm sorry, OK? I just want to get it right, I just – I'm going to do one more draft.

Fiona   You've done fifteen.

Alice   I need to check the spelling.

Fiona   Run spell-check.

Alice   I have. I need to check for stuff it missed.

Fiona   What stuff?

Alice   I don't know, that's why I need to check it! Writing this email's the most important thing I've ever done, I don't want it to open with 'Dear Mum and Dad, I've got something very important to tell you. I'm a Lebanon.'

Beat.

Look, Fee, it's late, they'll be in bed, can't we just wait?

Fiona   Till when?

Alice   I don't know, January?

Fiona   What, you mean in twenty-four hours?

Alice   Yes, maybe it can wait twenty-four hours.

Fiona   Fine. Fine. Wait twenty-four hours. That is absolutely fine.

Alice   Well, it obviously isn't, is it?

Fiona   No, it is. It's fine. And y'know why? It means I win the bet.

Beat.

Alice   No it doesn't.

Fiona   No?

Alice   No. No it does not – I didn't say I wasn't going to send it, I just said I wasn't going to send it tonight.

Fiona   There's a difference?

Alice   Yes! I am going to send it, OK? But even if I didn't, you still wouldn't win the bet, you'll never win the bet because I'll still come out before Angelina Jolie because Angelina Jolie is not a – No, y'know what, I'm not rising to this.

Fiona   Fine.

Beat.

Alice   She's married.

Fiona   Divorced.

Alice   She's been married.

Fiona   He's gay too.

Alice   She's been married several times.

Fiona   They're beards.

Alice   Lesbians don't have beards, gay men have beards.

Fiona   What do we get? Hair extensions?

Alice   They've had kids.

Fiona   Half of them are adopted.

Alice   Half of them aren't.

Fiona   She basically admitted to being gay in an interview.

Alice   She said she was bisexual!

Fiona   That's code!

Alice   Why would she use code?

Fiona   Because there are no lesbian film stars.

Alice   Yes, there are!

Fiona   No, no, there's one, and who guessed she was gay seven years ago?

Alice   Oh my God, you cannot use Jodie Foster in every argument! Yes, you said she was gay, but you say that about pretty much everyone else too, so you had to get it right at least once.

Fiona   Twice.

Beat.

I was right about you, wasn't I?

Pause.

Alice   I want to send it, OK? I do, I just . . . If I didn't, would that be so bad?

Fiona   I don't know. Do you want to stay here?

Beat.

Alice   I wouldn't mind.

Fiona   Really? You like it here?

Alice   Yes.

Fiona   You like Rotterdam?

Alice   Yes.

Fiona   *Waarom kun je me dan niet vertellen wat if nu zeg?*

Beat.

We've lived here seven years!

Alice   I'm not good at languages.

Fiona   You never tried to learn.

Alice   I work for an English company.

Fiona   An English company that's based in Holland.

Alice   Yes, and one that I can't just walk away from, actually, you can't do what I do just anywhere.

Fiona   Alice, there are ports in England, there's one in Hull two hundred miles that way!

Beat.

Alice   But we don't know anyone in England.

Fiona   We barely know anyone here. All the expat friends we had went home.

Alice   You'd have to leave your kids at school.

Fiona   They're only mine till June, you get new ones every year, that's kind of how being a teacher works.

Alice   What about your lesbian book club?

Fiona   Yeah, I'm pretty sure I can find some gay women in the UK who can read.

Beat.

Alice. Seven years.

Beat.

Alice   I know, I know, I will send it. OK? I will. I just . . . it's hard. You never had this problem, your parents didn't care, they've done drugs, they go on protests, they think the *Guardian*'s too reactionary.

Fiona   Alice. Your parents are fine. They must suspect something.

Alice   No. They don't. They think we're flatmates and you're too opinionated to get a boyfriend. I'm their only daughter, you don't know what they're like, this email could be the last piece of correspondence we ever have, so if I'm reluctant to send it . . . I know you're trying to understand but it's different for you, you came out at fifteen.

Fiona   Seventeen.

Alice   That doesn't matter! You're better at this than me. You've always known who you are, you've never felt like you had anything to hide, and that's not a bad thing, that's not a criticism, that's . . . why I love you.

Beat.

Fiona   Y'know, that's not true.

Alice   Yeah, I don't believe it either sometimes but I do.

Fiona   No, I mean . . . Look, if you don't want to send it, you don't have to. It's OK.

Alice   I know.

Beat.

Fiona   Come on, it's past midnight, it's New Year's Eve tomorrow, let's go to bed, yeah?

Alice   No. I . . . I want to send it.

Fiona   Seriously, you have to be up for work in seven hours.

Alice   I'm being serious. I want to send it.

Beat.

Fiona   You know you don't have to.

Alice   I know. I want to.

Fiona   Are you sure?

Alice   Yes. Yes. Yes I am. Would you . . . y'know . . .?

Fiona   What?

Alice   Read it.

Fiona   Really?

Alice   Yes. I want you to.

Fiona   OK.

Alice *hands* **Fiona** *the laptop.* **Fiona** *starts to read the email.*

Alice   I mean, it's rough but, I mean, I didn't want to over-think it so –

Fiona   Alice.

Alice   Sorry.

Silence.

Are you done yet?

Fiona   No.

A longer silence.

Alice   Well?

Fiona   Wait.

An even longer silence.

Fiona *puts the laptop down.*

Alice   Well? What do you think?

Fiona   I'm not quite done, I just had to . . . Wow.

Alice   Wow? Wow what?

Fiona   Wow . . . Just wow. You want my opinion?

Alice   Yes!

Beat.

Fiona   Bit gay.

Beat.

Seriously, no, I mean, it's good. It's really . . . good.

Alice   Really?

Fiona   Yeah, I didn't know you could write something like, y'know, what you wrote about me.

Alice   I meant it.

Fiona   I know.

Beat.

Alice   So is it alright?

Fiona   Yeah. Yeah, it's . . . perfect.

Alice   Thanks.

Beat.

I mean I'll run spell-check one more time. Y'know, just to be sure.

She does.

Beat.

Right. Done.

Fiona   You can check it again if you want.

Alice   I don't.

She picks up the laptop.

Right.

She goes to hit 'send'.

Fiona   Wait. Wait a second.

Alice   What?

Fiona   I . . . Nothing.

Alice   Nothing?

Fiona   Yeah, nothing, sorry, go on.

Alice   OK.

Beat.

Right.

Beat.

Here goes.

Alice *goes to hit 'send'.*

Fiona   Yeah, no, wait. No, there is something . . .

Alice   What?

Fiona   I don't really know how to . . . I don't –

Alice   Are you alright?

Fiona   Yes. No, no, I'm fine, I just . . . I –

Alice   What is it?

Fiona   Nothing, nothing, look, it's stupid, OK? Just send it.

Alice   No. Fee, what's wrong?

Fiona   Nothing. Nothing's wrong. I just . . . you said I didn't have anything to hide and –

Alice   And what?

Fiona   And then you wrote all that stuff about me and how you felt –

Alice   I thought you liked it.

Fiona   I did like it. Of course I liked it.

Alice   Then what's the problem?

Fiona   There isn't a problem. It's not a problem. It's just . . . there's something about me that you need to know, OK? Something I haven't told you, haven't told anyone.

Alice   What?

Fiona   I don't know how to say it.

Alice   Say what? Is it something you've done?

Fiona   No, no, it isn't anything I've done, I just –

Alice   It's alright, you can tell me –

Fiona   I know, Alice, please –

Alice   You can tell me –

Fiona   I think I'm a man.

Beat.

It sinks in, then HE *repeats.*

I think I want to . . . I think I'm meant to be a man.

Scene Two

Alice's *office.*

Alice *sits at her desk, reading something intently on her computer.*

Opposite her, **Lelani** *is bored.*

Silence.

Lelani   Where are you going tonight?

Alice   Hmm?

Lelani   Where are you going tonight? For *oudejaarsavond*?

Alice   Sorry, what?

Lelani   *Oudejaarsavond.* New Year. Where are you going?

Alice   Oh. Erm. Nowhere. Probably.

Pause.

Lelani   What are you doing then?

Alice   Hmm?

Lelani   What are you doing?

Alice   I don't know. Nothing.

Beat.

Lelani   Nothing?

Alice   Yeah.

Beat.

Lelani   But it's New Year.

Alice   What?

Lelani   It's New Year.

Alice   Yeah, I know.

Lelani   You cannot do nothing on New Year.

Alice   Well, I do.

Beat.

Lelani   I don't know anyone who does nothing on
New Year.

Alice   *No?*

Lelani   No. Back home, in Groningen, my friends, we
would always go out into the fields by my house, because it is
so dark you can see all the stars, and we'd walk out on the
canals, because they freeze over, and we'd just play music
and drink and set off fireworks. It is so much fun.

Alice   Right. Yeah, well, I don't really like fireworks.

Lelani   You don't like fireworks?

Alice   No.

Lelani   You don't like fireworks?

Alice   No.

Lelani   I have never met anyone who doesn't like fireworks.

Alice   Well, you just have.

Lelani   But everyone likes fireworks.

Alice   No, everyone in Holland likes fireworks. The rest of us know they're dangerous.

Lelani   But how do you celebrate New Year without fireworks?

Alice   *Safely.*

Beat.

Lelani, sorry but . . . haven't you got any work to do?

Lelani   No. Wouter took the day off. It's New Year. I'm pretty bored.

Alice   Right. Well, I do, so . . .

Pause.

Lelani   You know he tried to kiss me?

Alice   What?

Lelani   Wouter.

Alice   He tried to kiss you?

Lelani   Yah. At the *Sinterklaas* party.

Alice   He . . . I mean, he . . . Look, you know that's not OK, right? I mean, how old are you, twenty-two? Twenty-three?

Lelani   Twenty-one.

Alice   Twenty-one. Right, and he's your boss, he shouldn't have done that.

Lelani   Yah, but it's OK. I didn't kiss him back.

Alice   Right, yeah, that's not the point.

Lelani   He was like, 'Come on, just once', and I was like, 'No way! And if you try it again I'm going to tell my dad.'

Alice   What, does he know your dad?

Lelani   Yah, they are like best friends. That's why I got the job here. My parents were like, 'You've finished university you need to come and work with us,' and I was like, 'No way, I'm going to go and live in the city.' And they were like, 'No, we don't want you to do that,' and so I was like, 'I don't care, fuck you,' and then I came here on my own and called Wouter and he made me his assistant and let me come live with him.

Alice   Right. Wait, hang on, you live with Wouter?

Lelani   Yah. And his wife and kids. It's pretty awkward. But he doesn't charge me rent. 'Cause I think he's in love with me or something. But I am not interested. 'Cause he is really old. And I am gay.

Alice   Oh. Right.

Beat.

Look, Lelani, would you mind . . . It's just I've got these contracts to work on so . . .

Lelani   So what?

Alice   Would you mind being quiet?

Lelani   Oh. OK.

Pause.

Transsexuals?

Alice   What?

Lelani   On your computer. It says transsexuals. I can see the reflection in the window. It's been open the whole time.

Alice   What? Hey –

Lelani   What contracts are you working on?

Alice   That's not – that's – that's – that's just – just a pop-up.

Lelani   From what website?

Alice   From . . . a work . . . Wikipedia. It's nothing.

Lelani   It's still open.

Alice   Stop looking at my screen!

Beat.

It's just something I'm reading about, OK? Not for me. Not that it'd be a problem if it was. It just isn't. I've got . . . a friend and they are thinking about . . . I just wanted to read up on it.

Lelani   And what have you found out?

Alice   Nothing, you keep talking to me.

Beat.

Lelani   You know, if you wanted me to go you could have just said.

Alice   Yeah, I know . . . I was trying to be polite.

Lelani   OK. Well, next time you could just be honest instead.

Beat.

Would you like to go out with me tonight?

Alice   What?

Lelani   Would you like to go out with me tonight? In Rotterdam. For New Year.

Alice   Would I like to go out with you tonight?

Lelani   That is what I asked.

Alice   Right. Erm, thanks, I'm . . . I'm already –

Lelani   Doing nothing. That is what you said.

Alice   Right.

Lelani   I have never been out for New Year in the city before. Wouter invited me to go with him, but I do not really want to do that, and my friends and family are all in Groningen, so I am going out on my own. Unless you would like to come too?

Alice   Well, when I said that –

Lelani   You can say no.

Alice   No, it's not that I –

Lelani   You do not have to be polite.

Alice   I'm not being polite . . . I am doing nothing, I'm just . . . doing nothing . . . not on my own.

Lelani   Oh.

Alice   I'm staying in, with a friend. My . . . girlfriend. I have a girlfriend.

Lelani   Oh.

Alice   I mean it sounds great. But . . . I've just got a lot on my mind at the moment, y'know, I just need to –

Lelani   Finish reading about transsexuals.

Alice   Right. Yeah.

Lelani *writes the name of a bar on a piece of paper and gives it to* **Alice**.

Lelani   Well, if you change your mind, I'll be here till midnight.

Alice   Thanks. But I'll probably just . . .

Beat.

I really don't like fireworks.

Scene Three

A café.

Alice *is sitting at a table, waiting. She has a sandwich in front of her.* **Fiona** *arrives, flustered.*

Fiona   I'm sorry, OK? I'm sorry. There was traffic, I didn't know how long it would take me to get here, then there was nowhere to lock my bike – I'm sorry, alright?

Alice   It's OK.

Fiona   No, it's like, twenty-five to two.

Alice   I said it's OK. I expected it.

Beat.

Fiona   What?

Alice   I expected it.

Fiona   What does that mean?

Alice   What?

Fiona   What do you mean, 'you expected it'? Am I habitually late?

Alice   No, I didn't mean – No, I meant it's New Year's Eve, the buses are all – Look, I didn't know you were going to cycle – It wasn't a dig, OK?

Fiona   Right.

Beat.

He notices the sandwich.

Well. I take it you didn't order anything for me while you were waiting?

Alice   This is for you. I'm not hungry. They didn't have anything vegan so I got them to make it.

Beat.

Fiona   OK, stop it.

Alice   Stop what?

Fiona   Just act normally.

Alice   I am acting normally.

Fiona   No, if you were acting normally you wouldn't be sitting here calmly like this. I was late, very late, annoyingly late. It's twenty-five to two. You should be shouting at me or sulking, not buying me a specially made sandwich, what the fuck?

Alice   I don't understand, you're annoyed that I'm not angry?

Fiona   Yes, actually, yes.

Alice   Fine. I'll be angry. I'm very angry. Is that alright?

Fiona   Better.

Beat.

I'm not ill, OK? You don't have to treat me like I'm dying or something.

Beat.

Alice   I'm sorry.

Fiona   No, I'm – look, I didn't mean to . . . Let's just start again, OK?

Alice   OK.

Fiona   Thank you for the sandwich.

Alice   You're welcome.

Fiona   What's in it?

Alice   Avocado, carrot and red pepper hummus.

Fiona   Nice.

Alice   Yeah, well, I thought you'd like it.

Silence.

So. Do you . . . want to talk about it?

Fiona   What, the sandwich? I think we've pretty much covered it.

Alice   No. Not the sandwich.

Fiona   Yeah, I know. No, we don't have to –

Alice   It's fine, I want to, I mean, as long as you do. I did some reading. This morning. On the internet.

Fiona   Seriously, Alice, we don't have to –

Alice   I googled it.

Fiona   You googled it?

Alice   Yes, I googled it, and –

She takes out a notebook.

Fiona   Oh my God, are those notes?

Alice   I just wrote a few things down.

Fiona   You googled it and you took notes? Are you planning on writing an essay?

Alice   No. I just wanted to properly understand – look, I don't own any books on the subject, OK? And I just wanted to understand what might happen next.

Fiona   And you thought Wikipedia would tell you?

Alice   Well *you* haven't.

Beat.

Fiona   I tried to tell you last night. I don't really know . . . Look, I haven't really thought about this either, I just . . . I mean, I know there are procedures that some people have . . . But some people don't have them, some people don't have them at all, and I haven't seriously considered . . . I mean, even if I did . . . transition, which is what it's called,

I'd need to live as a man for at least, like, two years before I could actually consider anything like . . . And even if I did . . . I mean, it wouldn't be a huge change, would it? It wouldn't mean new clothes or much of a haircut. There'd just be . . . hormones.

Alice   And what effects would they have?

Fiona (*sarcastic*)   Well, they'd make me more feminine.

Beat.

Sorry. Look, it won't – It wouldn't . . . I think there might be some side-effects but mostly it'll just be, y'know, lower voice, facial hair . . . man stuff. And my periods would stop, so our bad moods wouldn't be in sync any more.

Alice   I read that it would make your . . . grow, so it's like a –

Fiona   Oh God, yes, no, yes, I don't know, but it wouldn't – I mean, I think it depends person to person how much – Look, it's not like one day I'd wake up with a massive –

Alice   No.

Fiona   I mean people can't even . . . use them, y'know? I think.

Alice   No?

Beat.

Would you want to, if you could?

Fiona   I don't know. That's kind of –

Alice   I'm just asking 'cause one of the websites talked about – it said that some trans-men? That is the right word, right?

Fiona   Yes. I think so.

Alice   Good, right, yeah. So it said that some trans-men feel it's important to express that they have a . . . even if they don't have one. And I mean, I know we've never really used . . . toys but –

Fiona   Oh Jesus Christ, Alice –

Alice   No, I just wanted to say that if you did want to – I mean I just want to get it all out in the open so if you did want to use a – a – a strap-on, then –

Fiona   Oh my God, Alice, I don't know if I want to use a strap-on, it's not at the forefront of my mind!

Alice   Well, I was just asking! I'm sorry, this is just a lot to take in and I don't really know what to say and I don't want to feel bad in a few months' time because we didn't talk about something right now!

Pause.

So, in terms of a name. You'd have to . . . I mean you wouldn't keep –

Fiona   Adrian.

Beat.

Alice   Adrian?

Fiona   Yeah, it's the name my parents would have given me if I were a boy. I mean, biologically a boy.

Alice   Right.

Fiona   It was my granddad's.

Alice   Yeah, no, that makes sense.

Fiona   You don't like it.

Alice   No, no, that's not . . . I'm just not used to it . . . Adrian. Adrian. Adrian Adrian Adrian. Adrian, Ade, Adie –

Fiona   Just Adrian.

Alice   Right.

Fiona   Are you OK?

Alice   I'm fine. I'm fine. I'm just . . . I'm fine.

Silence.

It's just . . . when were you . . . planning on . . . telling me?

Fiona   What do you mean?

Alice   I mean when were you planning on telling me about this?

Fiona   Well . . . last night.

Alice   No, that's when you did tell me. When were you planning on it?

Fiona   Well, I wasn't really planning on anything.

Alice   You picked out a name.

Beat.

Fiona   I wanted to tell you, OK? I just . . . I didn't know how you'd react.

Alice   You think I'd just pack my bags and go?

Fiona   No, of course not. I . . . I was scared. I wanted to say something. So many times. I just . . . Look, it's not like it was a light-bulb moment, y'know? Like suddenly I realised . . . I mean, I always thought I was gay. I mean, I was a tomboy, I liked girls, I thought, yeah, gay, that makes sense . . . But then bit by bit as I got older it didn't anymore . . . But, I mean, how do you tell someone that? I didn't know how to put it into words. I still don't. It's just this feeling. Like, every time I open my mouth, it's not my voice, or when I look in the mirror, it's just not quite me. And when I think about men, or see them, I just . . . I know that . . .

Beat.

It's not that I'm trying to change. I don't want to become a man. I . . . I think . . . I know . . . I already am one.

Beat.

Alice   And you're sure? I mean, absolutely sure?

Fiona   Yes.

Alice   But how – I mean how can you know for certain?

Fiona   I dream as one.

Beat.

In my dreams. I'm a man. Every time.

Alice   Since when?

Fiona   Since always.

Beat.

But you know this doesn't change anything between us. You do know that?

Alice   Yeah. No, I know, I know.

Beat.

I just . . . What does it make me?

Fiona   What do you mean?

Alice   I mean . . . what am I now?

Fiona   I don't understand.

Alice   Well, I mean, if you're a man, am I . . . straight?

Fiona   Of course not. I mean, I don't know. You're you.

Alice   Yeah, I know that, it's just, I mean, for the last ten years I've kind of been trying to work out who that is, so –

Fiona   Well, it hasn't changed.

Alice   No, but you have. I mean, who you are, I mean who I thought you were, I mean what I – Look, twenty-four hours ago, I thought I was gay. I am gay. So, I'm just trying to work out what this means for me.

Fiona   It doesn't have to mean anything.

Alice   But I'm not attracted to men – I mean other men.

Fiona   When we first got together you said you weren't attracted to women.

Alice   Yeah, I was in the closet, I was in denial, I've spent
the last seven years trying not to be in denial, and, I mean,
look, I don't want to make this all about me . . . But what do
I tell my parents now?

Fiona   What you already wrote.

Alice   What I already wrote?

Fiona   Yes, it was perfect.

Alice   Perfect? Fee, it said I was gay and in love with a
woman. At the very least I'm going to have to add a PS!
You're talking about becoming a man.

Fiona   No, not becoming a man, and I'm not telling you
this so you can use it as an excuse to stay in the closet.

Alice   I'm not using it as an excuse, I'm just finding this
quite hard to work out.

Fiona   You think I'm not?

Alice   I'm not saying you're not, but you've had more than
fourteen hours to take it in.

Pause.

Are you sure this is what you want? I mean, really sure? You
really want to do this? You want to become a man?

Fiona   No, Alice . . . I just want to stop trying to be a
woman.

Scene Four

The roof of **Alice**'s *office building.*

Alice *and* **Josh** *look out at the river.*

Josh   Y'know, I come up here every day. And every day I
look out at the river at the ships unloading, and I dunno, I
just think . . . you're not supposed to stay here. You're not
supposed to stay in Rotterdam. It's a port. Everything's

moving on, it's all just passing through, nothing's standing still. It's all on its way somewhere . . . else.

Beat.

Alice   And there's nothing I can say to change your mind?

Josh   Nope.

Alice   But you can't just go.

Josh   Well, no, I need to work out my notice and I've got two months left in the flat. But after that . . .

Alice   What about the girl you were seeing?

Josh   Yeah, that wasn't going anywhere.

Alice   But where are you going to go?

Josh   I dunno. Travelling. I think. I've been saving up for it, and now seemed like as good a time as any. I mean we were only supposed to be here for a year.

Alice   And what about me?

Josh   What do you mean?

Alice   Well, I'm gonna miss you, you dick. You're my best friend. Who am I going to talk to when you're gone?

Josh   Well, you're not going to be here either, are you?

Beat.

I mean, that's what you said. You said you were going to go straight home and send that email to your parents. So I can only assume that the reason we're up here on the roof, the reason you summoned me up from the IT department, is because you want to tell me that you actually did do that and that lo and behold they are absolutely cool with the fact that you're a massive dyke.

Alice   Yeah, I didn't send it.

Josh   No? I thought you were definitely definitely going to this time.

Alice   Yeah, well, it was probably the two definitelys that should have given away that I wasn't actually going to.

Josh   Do you want to talk about it?

Alice   No, not really. I don't want to talk about anything. It's a slow day in the office. I just wanted some company, OK? You don't have to go into deep meaningful conversation mode.

Josh   OK.

Pause.

He lets it hang.

Alice   But . . . Josh, look, this isn't about anything in particular, OK, so don't read into it, but . . . can I ask you a hypothetical question?

Josh   Hypotheticals are my speciality.

Alice   OK, well, say you were the sort of guy who goes out with women –

Josh   I am the sort of guy who goes out with women.

Alice   No, I know that, but, say you were that sort of guy, but then you met a man, and you were attracted to him too.

Josh   Are you trying to matchmake?

Alice   No. Say you met a guy, and you realised that you liked guys too, in fact you realised you liked guys exclusively. Say you realised you were gay. And you built yourself a life and an identity for yourself. But then . . . Well, do you think you could ever go back?

Beat.

Josh   Alice, have you met someone?

Alice   No. I'm not talking about me. I'm talking about you! Hypothetically!

Josh   Yeah, I've seen through your 'hypothetical' ploy.

Alice   It wasn't a ploy. I haven't met anyone. Obviously.

Josh   So why are you worrying about becoming a hasbian?

Alice   I'm not worried about becoming a hasbian. OK, I'm not attracted to guys, I'm gay. I am one hundred per cent sure of that.

Beat.

But that's the thing, I mean, can we ever be completely sure? Like, if you saw a girl in the street that you thought was hot but then you realised it was a man –

Josh   Yeah, doesn't happen a lot.

Alice   That doesn't matter. What I mean is . . . How can we ever know who we're really attracted to?

Beat.

Josh   Well, that's easy. It's whoever you think about when you masturbate.

Alice   I'm trying to be serious!

Josh   What? That's the only time you're properly honest with yourself. There are people and things you think of in the moment that you'd never admit to normally. It's only when you're cracking one out thinking about a hermaphrodite dwarf that you know for sure.

Alice   Right, yeah, but on a, y'know, deeper level . . . when you're with someone, you love the person, right? Not just . . . what they are.

Josh   Sure.

Alice   And, I know this is a weird question, but if Fee were a man, do you think we would still have got together?

Josh   But she's not.

Alice   No, but if she were.

Josh   Then you wouldn't be with her.

Beat.

Alice, I've got to get back to work. But tell your parents. I know you're scared. But you're not going to change. It's time to leave.

Beat.

'Cause if you could be with a man, you know you wouldn't have ever been with Fee in the first place, would you?

Beat.

You'd still be with me.

He exits. **Alice** *is left alone.*

Scene Five

De Hoogstraat (the high street).

Fiona *has come to shop.* **Josh** *is getting in the way. They are arguing.*

Josh   That's it? That's all I'm getting? Those are your parting lines? No 'good luck'? No 'I'll miss you'?

Fiona   What? It's not like we see each other that much anyway.

Josh   No, but more than if we were living in different countries.

Fiona   OK, well, what do you want me to say then?

Josh   I don't know, Fee, something nice?

Fiona   Like what?

Josh   I don't know, just something better than, 'Well, make sure you give back all the stuff you've borrowed.'

Fiona   You've borrowed a lot of my stuff!

Josh   I've got a few books.

Fiona   A lot of books. And DVDs. And a microwave.

Josh   That was Alice's, she gave me that.

Fiona   No, it was ours, and we didn't have room for it. It wasn't a gift, we were lending it.

Josh   She gave it to me on my birthday.

Fiona   No. We lent it to you on your birthday. OK? Now I've heard your news, thank you very much for letting me know, but if you don't mind, I need to get all the stuff for New Year before the shops shut, so if that's all?

Josh   Fine. Fine, I don't need to be here, I've got plans, I only called you 'cause – No, y'know what, forget it, I told Alice you wouldn't care.

Beat.

Fiona   You already told her?

Josh   Yes, actually, this afternoon, I mean I would have talked to you first but I didn't know it was going to be such a joyful experience.

Beat.

Fiona   How was she?

Josh   What do you mean?

Fiona   I mean was she alright?

Josh   What? About me leaving? No actually. Floods of tears, begging me to stay, what can I say? I have that effect on people.

Fiona   No, I mean, in general, was she alright in general?

Josh   Not really. I mean she's still freaking out. Obviously.

Fiona   Freaking out about what?

Josh   What do you think?

Beat.

You know you're not being fair on her. You've got to give her space, this a big thing.

Fiona   What are you talking about?

Josh   What do you think?

Fiona   She told you?

Josh   She didn't have to.

Fiona   She didn't have to?

Josh   Of course not, I know you, Fee, I know what you're like. You can't force her to come out.

Fiona   What?

Josh   If she's not ready to send that email you can't make her.

Fiona   Right.

Josh   It's not as easy for her as it was for you. She needs time, you can't make her tell them, do you understand?

Fiona   No, actually, can you say it again but just be a bit more patronising?

Josh   I'm not trying to be patronising, I am just trying to give you advice.

Fiona   Which I didn't ask for.

Josh   Yeah, but which you do need, 'cause if you keep on pushing her, you will push her away.

Fiona   Oh, what? And now suddenly you're the expert on keeping her?

Beat.

Josh I don't even know why I try with you any more.
Seriously. I don't even . . . I mean, you do know you won,
don't you? You got the girl. You beat me. You could just be a
bit more . . . grateful.

Fiona Grateful?

Josh Yes, grateful. When you two got together, I supported
you. A lot of people would have just freaked out and left. I
dealt with it.

Fiona And what? Do you want a medal? You didn't force a
gay girl to carry on going out with you. Is that what you're
saying?

Josh No –

Fiona You didn't, I dunno, take revenge on me, is that
your big boast?

Josh I just meant –

Fiona Josh, someone broke up with you and started going
out with someone else. Seven years ago. Get over it.

Josh Yeah, but it wasn't just someone else, was it? You're
not just anyone.

Pause.

Have you called Mum and Dad today?

Fiona Why?

Josh I don't know. To say hello. Ask how they are. Wish
them Happy New Year. Do you need a reason?

Fiona I'll do it at midnight.

Josh Midnight their time?

Fiona I'll call them!

Josh Good. They like it when you do.

Pause.

Fiona Josh, you know I didn't plan it. With Alice. I never –

Josh   I know. I'm sorry, I didn't mean to drag it all up. You know you never have to feel bad about that. If it hadn't been you it would have been someone else. She's gay. Kind of a spanner in the works for any heterosexual relationship. I mean, yeah, if I'd known what was going to happen I probably wouldn't have invited you to come stay but . . . Come on, just tell me you'll miss me and I'll leave you alone.

Fiona   Are you sure you'll miss me?

Josh   Course I will. I mean, I fucking hate you sometimes, but you're still my little sister.

Fiona *flinches.*

Josh   What? What's wrong?

Fiona   Nothing, nothing I just . . . Josh, there's something I need to tell you.

Scene Six

Alice *and* **Fiona**'s *flat.*

They are arguing. Their home phone is sitting between them.

Fiona   It's just a phone call. It's not a big thing.

Alice   But it's New Year's Eve.

Fiona   And?

Alice   You can't tell them on New Year's Eve.

Fiona   Why not? They won't be doing anything. They'll be at home watching TV. It's the same every year, Gran comes round and they watch Jools Holland.

Alice   But why do you have to do it right now? You know you don't have to come out to everyone in your life on the same day, you don't get points for efficiency. I mean, you don't know even how you're going to do it, you haven't written anything down, what are you going to say? 'Oh hi, Mum and Dad, I'm a man, happy New Year.'

Fiona   Why not? That's pretty much how I told them I was gay, I have done this before, y'know.

Alice   No, this is different, you know this is different. You don't know how they're going to react. I mean, do you really think you should be doing this over the phone?

Fiona   Alice, you were going to come out via email!

Alice   Yes, but only because I'd thought about it beforehand, and after thinking about it I decided that that would be the best way to do it.

Fiona   Yes, but then you never did it!

Alice   Yes, but only because I didn't know how they were going to react!

Josh *enters.*

Josh   Right. Guys. I did some more reading on my phone while in the toilet and I think I have found some options to look into.

Fiona   Josh, can this just wait –

Josh   No, no, hear me out, there's a clinic in The Hague that says you can email to arrange a consultation, they also say they'll try and find you an appointment within the week of booking, so if you do it now you could see someone as soon as Monday.

Fiona   I've got work on Monday.

Josh   Alright, some other day, or there's a place in Delft that have a drop-in clinic, and they're open some evenings –

Fiona   Great, that's great, just bookmark it.

Josh   Already done, and there's this forum on this website that has a list of all the online support groups you can join. TransAction, TransMission, there's even one for Catholics called TransSubstantiation. Not really, but it made me laugh when I thought about it.

Fiona   Josh. Seriously. I can do this myself.

Josh   I know, I know, I'm just, I'll email them to you, yeah?

Alice   Look, I'm not saying you shouldn't do it, OK? I'm just saying – I'm just saying that this afternoon you told me you wanted to take it one step at a time, now it seems like you want to take the whole staircase in one running jump. I mean you've told your brother, you're talking clinics, you've been shopping –

Fiona   The shopping wasn't my idea –

Josh   Yeah, that was me actually, I googled it and found this centre where –

Fiona   Josh.

Alice   Right, yeah, I know, I know, but what I mean is you've bought clothes, new deodorant, those things to flatten your chest.

Josh   The binders? It's called a binder.

Fiona   *Josh!*

Alice   A binder, right, yeah, sure.

Fiona   Alice, it's just a vest.

Alice   I know. I know it is, it's just . . . it's not something you'd even considered last night, and now you've got three of them.

Fiona   They were on offer.

Josh   Three for two.

Fiona   *Josh!*

Alice   It doesn't matter, it doesn't matter how many you've got, that's not the point, the point is I just think there's a lot of 'doing' going on at the moment and I can't help feeling like you're not taking any time to think things through.

Fiona   I've had my whole life to think things through!

Beat.

OK. Look, if it makes you happy, I'll write something down, OK? I'll get a pad, we can discuss it, we can have a conversation, and then I'll call them, is that alright?

Alice   Well, I don't . . . Yes. Fine. Whatever.

Fiona   Great.

Fiona *puts down the phone and exits.*

Pause.

Josh   So . . .

Alice   So.

Josh   Yeah. Big day. Big surprise. But not really shocking. It kind of adds up, y'know, like the end of *The Sixth Sense*. In a weird way. To me anyway.

Alice   Right. Josh. About what I said earlier. Just forget about it, OK?

Josh   Right.

Alice   I was just finding it all a bit, y'know, and I didn't know she was going to tell you right away, so, look, just please, forget I said anything.

Josh   Already done.

Beat.

But Alice, if you do feel that . . . y'know.

Alice   Just forget it. OK? She doesn't need to know.

Beat.

Josh   He. He doesn't need to know.

Fiona *re-enters with a notepad and pen.*

Fiona   Right. So, to begin with, 'Hi, Mum and Dad, I'm a man, Happy New Year.' Right?

Josh It's to the point.

Fiona Great. Sorted.

Alice Right. Yeah. Or maybe, something more like, what about . . . the dream thing. That thing you said to me about your dreams.

Fiona Yeah, sure, I'll mention that too.

Alice And that, y'know, you're still working it out yourself –

Fiona Right. OK.

Alice And I mean, just let them know that you're not rushing into anything, that you're taking things slowly, just one step at a time –

Fiona Do you want to write this yourself?

Josh Why don't you say something about that time when we were kids and we all went camping in the Lake District and you borrowed a bunch of my clothes so you could be Han Solo in the costume competition and then you didn't want to change out of them for, like, the rest of the week.

Beat.

Fiona What has that got to do with anything?

Josh I don't know. Was that not something to do with it?

Fiona I liked Han Solo, Josh. I was ten years old. I'd just seen *Star Wars*.

Alice Maybe tell them something about the fact that you're still the same person, that it doesn't change the way you feel about them, that it won't change your relationship.

Beat.

Fiona Alice, I think they'll know that.

Alice Well, actually you don't know what they'll think, Fee.

Fiona What, and you do?

Alice   No. But I'm just trying not to make any assumptions.

Fiona   And what assumptions do you think I'm making?

Alice   Nothing, it doesn't matter, just ignore me, write whatever you want.

Fiona   No, Alice, what do you think they're going to say?

Alice   I don't know, Fee, they might be upset, this might upset them.

Beat.

Josh   Hey, look, why don't we just move on to the next thing, yeah? Why don't you tell them about your new name?

Alice   I meant shocked. I didn't mean –

Fiona   I know what you meant.

Alice   I didn't mean anything!

Fiona   What do you want me to say, Alice? That I'm scared? Or worried they'll disown me? Or say they don't love me anymore? 'Cause that seems to be what you're going for.

Alice   Of course I'm not going for that –

Josh   Do you want to know what I think?

Fiona   Josh, please –

Josh   No, no, look, this is big and complicated, it's OK to feel apprehensive –

Fiona   Josh, we don't need you to explain it to us.

Josh   I'm not trying to explain it, just give a fresh perspective.

Fiona   What perspective? Sorry, am I forgetting the part of your life when you were born in a woman's body? 'Cause I lived with you for the first eighteen years, I think I probably would have noticed.

Josh   I am just trying to help, I am just trying to give you some advice.

Fiona   I don't need you to give me advice, I don't need either of you to give me advice, I don't need anyone to tell me what to do!

Alice   I'm not trying to tell you what to do, I just want you to slow down.

Fiona   Why? What difference is it gonna make? However they're going to react is how they're going to react, it doesn't matter how I phrase it, if they're going to get upset, there's nothing I can do about it, so I might as well do it now!

The phone starts ringing. They all look at it.

Josh *picks it up but doesn't answer it.*

Fiona   Is it . . .?

He nods, it's them.

Fiona *takes the phone off* **Josh**.

Fiona *looks at* **Alice**.

Alice *still doesn't want him to do it.*

Beat.

If he doesn't answer it now . . .

He answers it.

Fiona   Hello?

Yeah, hi Dad. Yeah, it's me.

Erm, yeah, happy almost New Year to you.

Yeah, they both say hi.

They do not both say hi.

Yeah, we're fine, everything's good, I just – Can you . . . Is Mum there, can you put her on?

Erm, no, I don't – not speakerphone, I don't – OK, speakerphone.

Hi Mum. Happy almost New Year to you too.

Oh no, no, nothing planned. Probably just staying in.

No, I don't need to . . .

Hi, Gran.

It's Fiona.

Fiona.

Don't worry, it's fine, just . . . can you put Mum back on, yeah? Mum. Judy. Your daughter. Can you put her . . . Thank you. Happy New Year.

Hey Mum, can you just –

Yeah, he's here, but can you just –

No, I'll put him on in a minute, I just . . . Are you both . . . Look . . . Can you just . . . sit down, OK? I've got something to . . .

No, I'm not actually, I'm not OK. There's something I . . .

No, I'm fine, I'm not ill, I'm fine, I'm . . .

Look, this is just a bit . . .

I'm trying to tell you, I'm just . . .

Do you remember that time we went camping in the Lake District and . . .

Mum, I think I'm transgender.

Beat.

Yeah, like, I'm a man, but born in a woman's body.

Yeah, they're both here, I've told them.

Beat.

Thank you.

I love you too.

Yeah, I know, I know that.

Yeah, yeah, I er . . . I want to start living as one, I think.

No, I don't need any money for anything, I'm alright.

I don't know. I don't really know what happens next.

Yeah, she's alright, I think, you're alright, aren't you?

Alice *is not alright.*

Fiona   No, I haven't told anyone else. You're all the first.

Adrian.

Yeah, after Granddad.

Out of sight to **Fiona**, **Alice** *goes to get her coat,* **Josh** *silently questions it.*

Fiona   I'm fine. I'm OK. I feel . . . relieved actually. Just . . . relieved.

And scared.

I know you are.

Josh *tries to silently ask* **Alice** *what she's doing but she just shakes her head. She needs to get out of there.*

Fiona   Look, it's all a bit . . . it's quite a lot to think about. Can I call you back in a bit? I'm really sorry for dropping this on you on New Year, it's all just . . .

Josh *gestures towards* **Fiona**. **Alice** *apologises silently, but she has to go.*

Fiona   I know.

I know.

Alice *exits.*

Fiona   I love you.

Goodbye.

He hangs up.

Beat.

(*Ironically.*) Well . . . turns out that was a piece of piss.

He sees that **Alice** *isn't there.*

He realises she has gone.

Beat.

Josh   She just . . . I think she just needed some fresh air. I'm sure she's just . . . y'know.

Fiona   Right.

Josh   It's been a big day. Probably just processing it all.

Fiona   Yeah.

Josh   I'm sure you don't have to worry. She'll be alright. She'll probably be back in a few minutes anyway. I mean, it's ten o'clock on New Year's Eve. Where's she even going to go?

Scene Seven

A bar.

Alice *is standing at a table.*

Lelani *enters and puts down two small glasses of amber liquid.*

Lelani   Here.

Alice   Oh, no, I was going to get these –

Lelani   It's OK. It's on me. *Bitterballen?*

She offers **Alice** *a bowl with some snacks in it.*

Alice   Are they vegetarian?

Lelani   Are you?

Alice   Well, yeah, I mean except for fish and chicken and
. . . meat – my girlfriend's pretty passionate and she does
most of the cooking.

Lelani   Oh, well, if you want them – *Eet smakelijk*. That
means enjoy.

Alice   Thanks.

Lelani *lights a joint.*

Alice   Are you allowed to do that in here?

Lelani   Yah. Look around.

Alice   Are we in a coffee shop?

Lelani   No. We are in a bar that lets you smoke.

Alice   Oh, right.

Beat.

She looks at the drink.

This isn't . . . I mean this is just alcohol, right?

Lelani   *Apfulkorn.*

Alice   Right.

She takes a sip and grimaces.

Lelani   No?

Alice   No, it's good, it's . . . got a bit of a kick.

Lelani   Yes, it does. Would you like?

She offers **Alice** *the joint.*

Alice   Oh, no, no, I'm fine. Thank you.

Lelani   OK.

Alice   I mean, I've never really – I had a hash brownie once
at a party. But it was an accident so I spat it out. I mean, I
know it's supposed to be relaxing, but I obviously don't need
any help with that.

Beat.

Actually could I just . . . give it a try?

Lelani   OK.

Alice *accepts it and takes a drag. She coughs. She grabs the* apfulkorn *and takes a swig. She grimaces while coughing.*

Lelani   Are you alright?

Alice   Fine.

Lelani   Here. Again. But this time, breathe, don't suck. So it goes in your lungs, not your stomach.

Alice   Right.

Alice *takes another drag.*

Lelani   See?

Alice *coughs, but just a bit.* **Lelani** *takes the joint.*

Alice   Thanks.

Beat.

I'm not feeling anything.

Lelani   It takes time.

Alice   Right.

Silence.

So . . .

Lelani   So.

Beat.

Why are you here?

Alice   What?

Lelani   Why are you here?

Alice   Oh, right, well, like I said, my girlfriend got held up, I can't stay, I was just –

Lelani   No, no, I know that. I meant why are you *here*. In Holland?

Alice *takes the joint back off* **Lelani**. *They pass it back and forth and take drags on it as they talk.*

Alice   Oh. Well, *that* is a good question.

Beat.

Lelani   Well, are you going to answer it?

Alice   Right, yeah, um, nothing exciting. I applied for a job here and got it.

Lelani   And did you come with your girlfriend?

Alice   Ah, no. On my own. Well. Actually. With a boy. A boyfriend.

Lelani   You had a boyfriend?

Alice   Yeah, it was complicated. Well, no it wasn't. No, actually it was, but y'know, we all have that awkward stage when we go out with men, don't we?

Lelani   No. I came out when I was ten.

Alice   Right. Well, I didn't. I met Fiona a few months after I moved here. One thing led to another and . . . weird, isn't it? That phrase. I don't really know how exactly one thing did lead to another. But it did. Anyway, that's me. Why are you here? Why Rotterdam?

Lelani   Duh, because it's the best city in the world.

Alice   Right.

Lelani   You don't think so?

Alice   Um . . . not in so many words.

Lelani   Then why are you still here?

Alice   Well, I . . . I really don't feel like this is doing anything for me at all actually, are you feeling it?

Beat.

I'm not out. To my parents. Or anyone. Anyone who's not here.

Lelani   Why not?

Alice   Because. I'm just not. They're not bad people. Look, who knows, they might even be fine with it, I just . . . I had this cousin who came out years ago and I just remember all my mum could say when she heard was . . . 'Oh, his poor parents,' like he'd died or something, and . . . and look, I just don't really like it here, OK? A lot of people don't like where they live. And I'm sure it's exciting when you're twenty-two, twenty-three.

Lelani   Twenty-one.

Alice   Right, yeah, but when you've been here seven years . . . I've kind of done it all now, y'know?

Beat.

Lelani   Except you have never smoked weed.

Alice   And?

Lelani   And you don't celebrate New Year.

Alice   What's that got to do with anything?

Lelani   And you don't know what *bitterballen* are, even though, I mean, they are served in every pub.

Alice   Well, they're not vegetarian so I wouldn't have had them –

Lelani   And you don't know enough people to have someone to meet up with for a drink on New Year.

Alice   That's not true.

Lelani   Then why are you with me? Alice, do you want to know what I think?

Alice   I don't know. No, probably not.

Lelani   I think you should take a shit or get out of the bathroom.

Alice   What?

Lelani   I think you should take a shit or get out of the bathroom! So you have not come out to your parents. Who cares? Your parents are not here. But you are. So have fun! Enjoy yourself! Enjoy living here! You cannot say you do not like it, you have never even tried it, you have been here seven years and you do not even speak Dutch!

Alice (*too defensively*)   And what has that got to do with anything?! No, really, I'm serious, have you ever actually tried to learn Dutch? In Holland? You can't! Everyone speaks English. You go into a shop and say *hoedemorgen*, they look at you and say, 'Oh, Engels, allow me.' You're too busy trying to prove you can speak our language to let us even have a chance of learning yours. And yeah, I don't celebrate New Year, and I haven't smoked a joint before – which by the way isn't working – you know what else? I don't like cheese, I don't wear clogs, I don't own any daffodils, I've never been in a windmill, I don't even know how to ride a bike! And you know why? Because I don't want to. I don't want to be here. I never did. But not all of us knew we were gay at the age of ten, OK? Some of us were more confused than that, some of us were confused for a very long time, some of us are still confused because every time we think we've got a handle on something, the one person we think we can count on comes in and tells us everything we thought was true in our lives, isn't! And I don't see how speaking Dutch would make any fucking difference there!

Beat.

She bursts out laughing.

She starts coughing. She picks up the apfulkorn *and downs it, then grimaces and retches while still coughing.*

She coughs even more.

Lelani   Oh, so you do like it then.

Alice   No!

They both laugh.

I'm such a mess.

Lelani   No. No. You are – oh, I don't know how you say – you are *prettig gestoord*. It means . . . 'pleasantly disturbed'.

Alice *laughs even more.*

Lelani   It does not translate well.

Alice   No, I think it's pretty spot-on.

They continue to laugh until they calm down.

Beat.

Lelani *gets up suddenly.*

Lelani   Come with me.

Alice   What?

Lelani   We're going to do something, come on.

Alice   What?

Lelani   Come on!

She leaves.

Alice   Hey, wait – Lelani!

She gets up to go, she grabs a few bitterballen *and stuffs them in her mouth, then follows* **Lelani** *out of the bar.*

Scene Eight

A frozen canal.

Lelani *is walking out on to the ice, it crackles beneath her feet.*

Alice *is standing on the side, still quite stoned.*

Alice   I'm not going out there!

Lelani   Oh, come on.

Alice   Do you know how dangerous that is?

Lelani   Not at all.

Alice   People drown in canals all the time –

Lelani   It's been frozen for days. It's not going to crack.

Beat.

Alice?

Beat.

Are you going to leave me out here on my own?

Beat.

Alice   Fine. Fine, but if anything happens –

Lelani   Nothing's going to happen.

Alice   Fine.

She lowers herself on to the canal as **Lelani** *lights up another joint.*

She slowly and unstably walks towards **Lelani**.

Lelani   It's OK. It's OK. See? Here you are.

Alice *stands on her own.*

Alice   Right. Right. This is great.

Beat.

Can we go back now?

Lelani   No. Hold this.

She hands **Alice** *the joint.*

Alice   I don't think I need any more –

Lelani   I know, just hold it.

Alice *takes the joint.* **Lelani** *takes off her bag, puts it on the ice, opens it up and takes out several small firecrackers.*

Alice   What are you doing?

Lelani   Duh. It's New Year, I'm not letting you go home until you've set off a firework.

Alice   What? No! No, I don't want to – what if it cracks the ice?

Lelani   It's not going to crack the ice. Here, look.

She lights one of the firecrackers and throws it away down the canal.

It lands and explodes.

See?

Alice   I still don't think –

Lelani   Alice. Do you know what we call tonight?

Alice   New Year's Eve?

Lelani   No. *Oudejaarsavond.* Old Year. It's not the new one until tomorrow. So try it. And if you don't like, you can leave it behind with everything else.

Beat.

Alice   Fine. OK. Fine. Give me the –

Lelani *hands* **Alice** *a firecracker, then holds up her lighter.*

Lelani   As soon as you see sparks, throw it.

Alice   OK.

Lelani *tries to light it.*

Lelani   Not yet.

It sparks.

Now, now!

Alice   What, just – ?

Lelani   Yes!

Alice *lets out a yelp as she throws it.*

It lands a few metres away and then explodes.

Alice   Oh my God.

She laughs.

Lelani   See?

Alice   Oh my God.

Lelani   Did you like it?

Alice   No!

Beat.

Can I do it again?

Lelani   Of course.

She takes another firecracker and hands it to **Alice**.

Lelani *tries to light it.*

Alice   Now?

Lelani   Wait.

Alice   Is it – ?

Lelani   I'm just trying to –

Alice   Is it –

Lelani   Yes, yes, now, throw it, throw it.

Alice *drops it.*

Alice   Shit, shit!

Lelani   It's OK, just –

She picks it up quickly and throws it.

It explodes harmlessly a few metres away from them.

Alice   I'm sorry, I'm sorry, I didn't mean to –

Lelani   It's OK. It's fine.

Alice   Oh my God, oh God, oh God, just – Give me that.

She snatches the joint off **Lelani** *and takes a large drag. She immediately starts coughing again.*

Lelani   OK, come here, give it to me.

She takes the joint off **Alice**.

Lelani   Here, let me show you, just, here, cup your hands around your mouth. Like this.

She demonstrates. **Alice** *copies her.*

Lelani   Right, Now, all you need to do is just breathe in, OK?

Alice   All I need to do when?

Lelani *takes a long drag of the joint.*

She cups her hands over **Alice**'s *and puts her face into them.*

Their mouths very close, she breathes the smoke out for **Alice** *to inhale.*

Then they part.

Lelani   Good?

Alice *nods weakly.*

Beat.

Lelani   Come out with me tonight.

Alice   What?

Lelani   Come out with me. Tonight. In Rotterdam.

Beat.

Alice   I . . . I can't.

Beat.

I have to go home. Sorry, I'd like to. Really.

Lelani   You are not just being polite?

Alice   No, I'm not just being polite.

Lelani   It's fine. There will be other times.

Alice   I don't know about that . . .

Lelani   Why not?

Alice   I don't think I'm going to be here much longer.

Lelani   Why? Are you going to tell your parents and go home?

Alice   I think I have to.

Lelani   No. You could tell them and stay.

Beat.

Gelukkig nieuwjaar, Alice. That means happy New Year. And *tot ziens*.

Beat.

That means I'll be seeing you.

Alice *hesitates for a moment . . . then leaves.*

Lelani *walks off along the ice.*

Scene Nine

Alice *and* **Fiona***'s flat.*

The TV is on. **Alice** *enters.* **Fiona** *has been waiting for her.*

Fiona   Are you OK? I was getting worried.

Alice   I'm fine. I was just . . . walking. Had a drink. The trams had stopped so it took me a while to get back . . . How long till midnight?

Fiona   A few minutes.

Beat.

Josh went out, he had friends waiting. And I wanted some time on my own so . . .

Alice   Yeah.

Fiona   I had a lot to think about.

Alice   Me too.

Beat.

She notices a vest-like item of clothing next to **Fiona**.

Alice   So, is that . . . what was it called? A . . . what was it?

Fiona   A binder.

Alice   Right. Have you tried it?

Fiona   No. No, I haven't.

Beat.

Alice   Are you . . . going to?

Fiona   Not if you don't want me to.

Alice   Oh, no, you can, I mean, it's fine, you probably should. I mean, as long as it doesn't set your eczema off.

Beat.

You can try it.

Beat.

Fiona   Would you . . . ?

He gestures for **Alice** *to help.*

Alice   Oh, right, yeah, course. Just let me . . .

She picks up the binder.

Fiona *takes off his shirt and hands it to* **Alice**.

He then takes off his bra and discards it on the floor without a second thought.

He takes the binder from **Alice** *and puts it on.*

He then takes the shirt back off **Alice** *and puts that back on.*

Fiona   Well, how does it look?

Alice   It works.

Beat.

Fiona   Alice, are you OK with this? 'Cause you know if you're not –

Alice   No. No, I am. I am. I'm here for you. You know that.

Fiona   I know.

Alice   I love you, Fee.

Fiona   I know, I –

Beat.

It . . . It wouldn't be Fee any more. My name. I mean, the name I want to . . .

I want to be called Adrian now.

On a nearby clock tower the chimes of midnight begin as the people on TV start to count down from ten.

Can you . . . Is that OK?

Beat.

Alice   OK.

Beat.

I mean yes, yes, it's . . .

Beat.

Adrian.

Beat.

Adrian.

The church bell strikes twelve and the countdown gets to one.

There are cheers from the people on TV.

Outside, thousands of fireworks are set off simultaneously.

End of Act One.

Act Two: Koningsnacht

Scene One

Alice *and* **Adrian***'s flat.*

Adrian *is shouting at someone in the next room.*

He has begun his transition and although he is not all the way there, he is now presenting as a man.

Adrian I'm not saying you actually had to do anything! I didn't want you to shout at him or wrestle him to the ground! I just think it'd be nice if sometimes you took my side when someone does something like that. 'Cause it's not like I enjoy it, I don't like it when something like that happens. But it does happen. It happens a lot. And when it does I'm not just going to let them get away with it, alright? I'm going to do something about it, I'm going to say something, and if you have a problem with that – which you shouldn't – but if you do, don't just storm off – which was great by the way, thanks very much, very supportive – if you have a problem, talk to me! Talk to me about it. If you think I acted like a dick, tell me I acted like a dick! We can have a conversation! We can have a fucking conversation like two grown-up adults!

Alice *enters. She's dressed all in orange from head to toe, including a hat and shoes.*

Adrian What is that?

Alice What?

Adrian What are you wearing?

Alice I'm going out.

Adrian Dressed like that?

Alice It's what everyone's dressed like.

Adrian You look ridiculous.

Alice   So does everyone else then.

Adrian   No, everyone else does not look like that, you look like you've been Tangoed.

Alice   It's King's Night. You're supposed to wear orange.

Adrian   No. Dutch people are, Dutch people who like the Dutch king.

Alice   I like the Dutch king.

Adrian   No you don't, you don't even like our royal family. You hated the Jubilee.

Alice   No, you hated the Jubilee, I don't like Paul McCartney. Now can I go please?

Adrian   No. I want to talk about what just happened.

Alice   Well, I don't have anything to say about it.

Adrian   I do!

Alice   Then phone a friend. Blog about it. I don't care.

Adrian   Do you not even want to talk about what the doctor said?

Alice   No. If you wanted to talk about what the doctor said, you could have talked to me about it on the way home, instead you decided to make what just happened, happen. And now, I've got to go, I'm late.

Adrian   It's only half five.

Alice   Yes, and everything started at two. I've already lost three and a half hours visiting a doctor and getting into a fight!

Adrian   It wasn't a fight.

Alice   Fine! It wasn't a fight, I don't care! I've told you, Fee, I don't want to talk about it!

Beat.

Sorry, it just slipped out.

Adrian   Whatever. It's fine.

Alice   No it's not. Adrian, I'm sorry.

Beat.

OK, five minutes. You've got five minutes, we can talk about it.

Adrian   No, it doesn't matter.

Alice   I'm saying we can.

Adrian   I thought you had to go.

Alice   Five minutes.

Beat.

Now what do you want to say?

Adrian   I don't want to say anything.

Alice   Well, it's going to be a long five minutes because I don't either.

Adrian   Yes you do.

Alice   I really don't.

Adrian   Just say it.

Alice   Say what?

Adrian   You know what.

Alice   No, the only person who thinks I have something to say is you, so unless you tell me what it is, I'm not going to say it.

Adrian   Say I overreacted.

Alice   No.

Adrian   But that's what you think.

Alice   No. If I thought you overreacted, I'd say you overreacted, I don't think you overreacted, so I'm not going to say it.

Adrian   I know when you're angry with me.

Alice   Why would I be angry with you?

Adrian   Because you think I overreacted.

Alice   I've just told you, I don't think you overreacted, and even if I did, you obviously don't, so what does it matter if I do?

Adrian   So you do?

Alice   I didn't say that!

Adrian   But you do, don't you?

Alice   Yes, of course I do! You did. You tried to start a fight with a man dressed as a giant orange lion! Does that sound like a particularly measured response?

Adrian   Well, what was I supposed to do?

Alice   Ignore him! He was dressed as a lion! It looked like you were picking a fight with Mufasa.

Adrian   What, so I should just let him get away with what he said?

Alice   What? *Dames gaan voor*? It was a mistake, he didn't realise!

Adrian   It wasn't a mistake, but even if it was, it's still sexist.

Alice   It's not sexist, it's polite.

Adrian   It's demeaning.

Alice   Saying 'ladies first' is not demeaning! And what did he say when you corrected him? '*Het split mij, Ik dacht dat je een vrouw was.*' It was a mistake. He apologised.

Adrian He'd been looking right at me, he knew what he was doing.

Alice He had a lion head on! He was looking at you through the mouth!

Adrian It was a big mouth! He could see me.

Alice Fine, he could see you, that still doesn't mean you have to yell at him in front of a whole crowd of people. I mean, look, I know the hormones make you angry, but –

Adrian Oh, don't blame the hormones. That's like me blaming your period. I'm not angry because of the hormones. I'm angry 'cause he was looking right at me and he still called me a woman!

Alice And? Until very recently you were!

Beat.

Adrian I wasn't a woman. I was a man.

Alice I know, I didn't mean –

Adrian I didn't use to be a woman. You wouldn't say someone 'used to be straight'.

Alice I meant before you transitioned, I meant physically, I meant – no, y'know what, you know I didn't mean it like that!

Adrian Then you shouldn't have said it.

Alice I shouldn't have said anything!

Adrian You don't understand.

Alice No. No, I don't. I don't understand. I mean, I go to the doctor's with you 'cause I enjoy hearing about mastectomies and scrotoplasties but I know that whatever I say is worthless 'cause I do not understand. That's why I don't say anything when you boycott the cinema 'cause a guy at the popcorn stand pointed you towards the women's toilets rather than the men's, or when you quit your lesbian book club because you decided you weren't eligible for membership any more – you, not them – or when you did what you did just now, 'cause yeah, I do think you overreacted, but what do I know? If you want to pick a fight with a lion? So what? I don't care. And why not call him a *kankerlijder* in front of a group of small children while you're at it – which is like the equivalent of saying cunt – 'cause if that's what you feel you have to do then that is absolutely fine with me. The only thing I will say, is that next time you do feel like doing something like that, just give me a little bit of warning beforehand so I can get off the tram first!

Beat.

You just have to be more patient with people.

Adrian   Oh, thanks, that's really what I need, one more person telling me to be patient, 'cause I don't hear that enough. 'Just be patient, Adrian.' 'The hormones'll work in time, Adrian.' 'The acne'll clear up and your voice will even out and you'll be ready for surgery but not just yet, Adrian.' So just be patient. Give it a bit more time.

Alice   You do need to give it time.

Adrian   I'm giving it time!

Alice   You didn't even give your kids time, you just expected no one to say anything and when one of them asked if you had a willy you quit.

Adrian   I didn't quit 'cause he asked me, I quit because the school didn't want me to sit down and talk to him about it!

Alice   Because he's six!

Adrian   The perfect age to learn.

Alice   It's a Christian school!

Adrian   That's not an excuse! Why do you never take my side? Why do you never support me?

Alice   Never support you? I'm still here aren't I?

Adrian   Yeah, you are, we both are, we're both still here.
We said we'd be gone by February, now it's nearly May.
When are we going home, Alice?

Alice   Oh my God, are you just trying to have all your
favourite arguments at once?

Adrian   That's not an answer.

Alice   Yeah, because I don't have time for this.

Adrian   That's what you said last time! That's what you say
every time!

Alice   I'm late.

Adrian   When are we going home?

Alice   I can't just leave like that. I have a job! I have work!

Adrian   Fuck work!

Alice   I can't 'fuck work', we haven't got the money, I've got
an overdraft, we've got your medication –

Adrian   It's covered by insurance.

Alice   Which I pay for.

Adrian   And you wouldn't have to if we had the NHS.

Alice   Fee –

Adrian   Adrian!

Alice   It was a slip of the tongue!

Adrian   Which you always make.

Alice   Accidentally! It was an accident. It's like calling your
teacher mum!

Adrian   Well maybe it wouldn't happen at all if you used
my real name!

Alice   I do use your real name!

Adrian   When?! You can barely say it! You hate it! You wince whenever I make you.

Alice   That's not true!

Adrian   And you don't let me touch you any more.

Alice   What?

Adrian   We haven't had sex in months.

Alice   Oh for fuck's sake!

Adrian   Two months. I've counted.

Alice   I've been busy!

Adrian   It's 'cause of what happened last time, isn't it?

Alice   I don't want to talk about last time.

Adrian   I didn't force you to do that. You said you'd give it a try!

Alice   I did give it a try! But there's giving it a try and giving it a try.

Adrian   And what's that supposed to mean?

Alice   It means I don't want to suck on the end of a dildo like it's your penis. OK? I don't want to touch it. I don't want it inside me. And I don't have to justify that, I just don't want to do it!

Adrian   And what are you going to do when there's a real one there?

Alice   I don't know, I thought you didn't want one!

Adrian   I don't know if I want one! Every time I try and talk about it you change the subject! But even if I did what would be the problem? I'm a man, why can't I have a penis?!

Josh *enters.*

Josh   OK, guys, maybe we should just all . . . calm down, yeah?

Beat.

Adrian   What are you doing here?

Josh   I was just in my room. *Because I live here now.* Don't worry, I had headphones on. Definitely didn't hear anything that will mentally scar me for life. I just thought maybe you could both use a time out.

Adrian   We're fine.

Josh   OK. Cool. Well, if either of you do want to grab a drink, I'm going to head to the pub, you're welcome to join.

Adrian   We're kind of in the middle of something.

Alice   Actually I think we're finished.

Beat.

Adrian   Fine. Fine. (*To* **Josh**.) Come on then.

Beat.

(*To* **Alice**.) I'll see you tomorrow.

Adrian *leaves.*

Beat.

Alice   I'm sorry. I didn't know you were there.

Josh   It's fine. Probably good I stepped in when I did. It was getting quite heated.

Alice   Yeah, I'm sorry about that too.

Josh   It's OK. Not a problem.

Alice   I'm just finding it all a bit much, y'know?

Josh   Yeah. I heard.

Beat.

So. On your way out?

Alice   Yeah, there's some people from work . . .

Beat.

Josh   Is one of them that Dutch girl?

Alice   What?

Josh   At work, there's a girl. I saw you with her a few times. Before I left. Is she . . . one of the people?

Alice   Well, yeah, yeah, she's one of them.

Josh   Right. Well. Have fun.

He leaves.

Beat.

Alice *sighs, takes off the hat and sits down.*

Scene Two

A pub.

Adrian *and* **Josh** *are standing holding pints.*

Adrian   I'm not asking people not to be confused. You know that, don't you?

Josh   Yeah.

Adrian   I'm just asking them to look at me and think for a second about how I am presenting myself. I'm obviously trying to present as a man, whether it works or not, that's obviously the intention.

Josh   I know.

Adrian   So if they can see that, if they can see I want to be treated like a man, I don't understand why they still choose to treat me like a woman.

Josh   'Cause they're idiots. Ignore them.

Adrian   But I can't. I can't just ignore them. It's everyone. It's everyone, all the time, and the one person doing it the most . . .

Beat.

Josh   I know. But it'll get better. It will. Now, come on, drink up. That'll put hair on your chest.

Adrian   Are you going to say that every time you buy me a drink?

Josh   Only till I stop finding it funny.

Beat.

Look, Ade, even if there are dickheads in the world, there's also people who are here for you. Me. Mum and Dad, I mean, they love that you're trans, it's given them a whole new set of marches to go on. And we're getting on much better now than we ever did as brother and sister, aren't we? Alice . . . she just needs time. I know it's hard, but . . . Think about tonight, a few years ago, King's Night didn't exist. It was Queen's Night for like a hundred years. Then the Queen stood down and her son took over, suddenly it's King's Night. And yeah, at first I'm sure people were confused, maybe they found it hard to adjust, one or two probably called it Queen's Night by accident, y'know, force of habit. But then they got used to it being King's Night, they saw that underneath nothing had really changed, and now they can barely remember when it wasn't.

Beat.

Adrian   I'm not a national holiday.

Josh   It's a metaphor.

Adrian   Yeah, well, not a very good one.

Josh   I'm just trying to help.

Adrian   Well, thanks very much, but weren't you supposed to be going travelling or something?

Josh   Yes, and I've already worked out my notice, as soon as you don't need me here anymore, I'm gone.

Adrian   Josh, I do know it was Alice who asked you to stay.

Josh   Yeah, well, you're the reason I did.

Beat.

She'll come round. Trust me.

Beat.

And in the meantime, maybe you do need to . . . I dunno, just learn to get better at . . . letting things go, yeah?

Adrian   Letting things go?

Josh   Yeah, y'know, just, like, when something happens ... I mean, look, obviously it's important that people see you as a man but, well, do you remember when you first came out as gay? You dyed your hair, bought Doc Martens, started watching *The L Word* on DVD.

Adrian   That was your DVD, I got that off you.

Josh   Yes, I know, we all liked *The L Word*, it's just . . . For a while everything became about being gay, and if anyone said anything wrong – I mean, you had a half-hour argument with your geography teacher 'cause he made a joke about the Isle of Lesbos – And, look, I don't think this counts as mansplaining 'cause you're a guy too. And I am very much checking my privilege as I say this. But . . . when someone says something like 'ladies first' . . . is it really worth getting that upset over?

Beat.

Adrian   Yes.

Josh   Right. Yeah, no, you're right. Ignore me. I stand corrected.

Beat.

Y'know this would be a lot easier if everyone in the world just treated everyone else the same.

Adrian   What?

Josh   I mean, none of this would be a problem if we didn't treat women like women and men like men.

Adrian   Yeah, it's called feminism, Josh, welcome to the party.

Josh   No, I know that, what I mean is, look, I know it's easy for me to say 'cause I'm – what's that word when your body and gender match up?

Adrian   Cis.

Josh   Right, yeah, I'm cis. (*A play on words occurs to him.*) Bro. But, what I'm trying to say is, it's society that teaches men and women to be different, isn't it? I mean we've got different bodies but there's no reason why men should, I dunno, like football more than knitting, but –

Adrian   Wait, stop, is that the best you can do? Football and knitting?

Josh   They're just examples, that's not the point, the point is, you want people to treat you like a man, right? But what does that even mean? Y'know? It's just a label. Like, if things were different, if we all lived in, like, I don't know, a dark cave or –

Adrian   A dark cave?

Josh   Yeah, like, where we couldn't see each other –

Adrian   And why do we live there?

Josh   I don't know, but if we were, if we were raised there –

Adrian   By who? Who's raising us in this dark cave?

Josh   I don't know, but if they did –

Adrian   Wouldn't we all have a vitamin D deficiency?

Josh   *If they did,* and we couldn't see we were different, and we didn't have a society that made us treat men like men and women like women, would we even have those names at all?

Beat.

Adrian   Yes.

Josh   No, we wouldn't, 'cause we're all the same. Listen –

Adrian   No, we're not. Josh. If we're all the same, how do you explain me? Well? Society taught me to be a woman too, didn't it? You were there, Mum and Dad taught me to be a girl, you to be a boy, right? So what went wrong? 'Cause that's not how I turned out. I'm a man. I am a straight man in a woman's body. I'm not saying it's that cut and dry for everyone, it probably isn't. And I'm not saying I wouldn't want to live in a world where we treated everyone the same. This dark cave sounds great. But we don't. We live in this world. We still use the words he and his. And all I'm asking is that while they still exist I want them to be used about me. I want to be asked to give my seat up on a bus. I want to use the gents. When a band asks all the men to sing along, I want to sing along. I don't want to change the world. I just want people to see me the way I want to be seen. The way I am.

Beat.

Josh   Well. I see you that way.

Adrian   Sure you do.

Josh   What? I do.

Adrian   Josh. I love you. But don't think I don't know, at the back of your mind . . . I'm still your little sister.

Beat.

It's alright. You're trying. It's more than most.

Beat.

My round.

He gets up and goes to get more drinks.

Scene Three

Alice *and* **Adrian**'s *flat.*

Lelani *enters,* **Alice** *follows.*

Lelani   So this is where you live?

Alice   Lani, what are you doing –

Lelani   I imagined it bigger.

Alice   You should have called – You –

Lelani   And it's not very clean.

Alice   Lani, what are you doing here?

Lelani   No, Alice, what are *you* doing here? *Godverdomme*, what is this shit?

Alice   I explained –

Lelani   No. You sent me an SMS. A text! When you're already half an hour late, I was already on De Hoogstraat, I had already bought you a drink –

Alice   I know, I'm sorry –

Lelani   And you did not even tell me the truth!

Alice   Yes, I did.

Lelani   Oh yeah? So where is she then? This girlfriend. The girlfriend you are spending the night with.

Alice   She's just . . . out. But she's coming back – Look, I wanted to come but we had an argument.

Lelani   So? You always argue, Alice, that is all you ever do together.

Alice   Yeah, well, this one was serious.

Lelani   And? It's *Koningsnacht*, Alice. It's the biggest night of the year. You said you wanted to spend it with me.

Alice   I know, and I did, I do, but . . . it's complicated.

Lelani   That is what you always say.

Alice   Yes, because it's always true!

Lelani   OK then, what was it about? This argument?

Beat.

She shakes her head and goes to leave.

Alice   No, wait, it was about me. It's what it's always about. It was about me. And that we're still here. And that she wants to leave and that . . .

Lelani   And that you don't? You do not want to go?

Beat.

Well, it's still not OK.

Beat.

Nice outfit though. Very Dutch.

Alice   You said wear orange.

Lelani   I did.

Alice   Is it too much?

Lelani   Yes.

Beat.

But you still look good.

Alice   Thanks. You too.

Lelani   I know.

Beat.

She notices **Josh***'s shoes.*

Lelani   I didn't know you lived with a boy.

Alice   What?

Lelani   Your girlfriend. She has big feet.

Alice   Oh, they're not hers, they're Josh's.

Lelani   Josh?

Alice   A friend. He's staying.

Beat.

Lelani   You know, I was actually really pissed off with you tonight.

Alice   Yeah, I gathered.

Lelani   This is my first *Koningsnacht* in the city. There are bands playing, they have a carnival, everyone is dressed up. It was going to be really fun.

Alice   I know, I know, I wanted to come.

Lelani   Then who is stopping you?

Beat.

Alice, do you know why people dress up tonight? Do you know why they wave flags, and wear orange, and shout 'hup Holland'?

Alice   No, but I assume you're going to tell me.

Lelani   Because they are proud. I do not understand why you are not allowed to do the things you want to do. If you want to stay here in Holland, stay. If you want to tell the truth to your parents, just do it. And if you want to come out with me tonight . . . I am right here. It's *Koningsnacht*. Tonight is about feeling proud of who you are. Don't you want to be part of that?

Beat.

Alice   Of course I do, I just . . . I can't. I'm sorry, Lani, I wanted to come. Honestly. I really did. And I'm not just being polite.

Beat.

Lelani   Well, it's OK.

Beat.

I could always stay here instead.

Alice   Ha, yeah, well, I don't know if that's a good idea.

Lelani   Why not?

Alice   Well . . .

Lelani   Well? What's the problem?

Alice   Well, there's no problem, it's just, my girlfriend, she . . .

Lelani   She does know about me, doesn't she?

Alice   Well, yeah. Of course.

Lelani   What does she know?

Alice   What?

Lelani   What have you told her?

Alice   I don't know, that . . . I'm friends with some of the girls at work.

Lelani   What, and I am just one of the girls?

Alice   Well, no, I mean, I may not have mentioned you by name, specifically.

Lelani   Oh. So I am a secret?

Alice   What? No.

Lelani   But you haven't told her about me. Even though we spend quite a lot of time together, no? We go for drinks most nights, we are friends. Good friends, yes?

Alice   Yeah.

Lelani   Then why haven't you told her?

Alice   I don't know.

Lelani   Are you sure?

Beat.

Oh my God, I don't know why you can't just say it.

Alice   Say what?

Lelani   What we are doing here. What this is. I think you know. You know what I want. You know why I am here. You know why, even though I could have spent tonight with anybody, I chose you. I could have gone home, I could have seen friends, I could have gone to a bar and found someone else. But I wanted to spend *Koningsnacht* with you. Why do you think that is?

Beat.

Alice   I . . .

Adrian (*off*)   Are you in?

He enters.

He sees them both.

Oh.

Beat.

I just stayed for two. (*To* **Lelani**.) Hello.

Alice   Oh, sorry, um, this is –

Lelani   Lelani.

Alice   Yeah, she's – I mean we – we work together.

Adrian   Right.

Alice   And, er, Lelani, this is . . . this is . . .

Lelani   Josh. No? You are staying? Alice said.

Adrian   Oh. Right, no, I'm –

Lelani   I was just leaving. (*To* **Alice**.) Well, you know where I'll be if you want me. *Tot ziens*, Alice. Goodbye, Josh.

She exits.

Pause.

Alice   She was . . . She just came round to . . . I . . . Are you OK?

Adrian (*quietly*)   I passed.

Alice   What?

Adrian   She just . . . I mean, you just saw – She just looked at me and . . . I passed.

Alice   What?

Adrian   She thought I was a man. She just accepted it. She just looked at me and . . . That was it. That was the moment. That was the moment I've been waiting for for . . . for ever. She just looked at me and she didn't even question it. Alice, I passed.

Alice   Yeah, right, I'm sorry –

Adrian   No, no, you don't – I'm sorry, Alice, Christ, I'm so sorry. I mean, I've been a prick, I know I have, I've been a prick to you for months, I know I've been trying to move fast, but it's just because . . . because I've dreamt of that moment! I've dreamt of that moment for so long, and you've been there, you've been there for me the whole time, and I've never said thank you, I never told you how much it means to me, I never told you how much you mean, and . . . Alice, I want to marry you.

Alice   What?

Adrian   I want to marry you. I mean, shit, I meant to do this with a ring – I was gonna wait until we went home, I've

been thinking about it for months, but – Jesus, let's just go.
We'll leave, we'll go tomorrow, we'll go and then we can
spend the rest of our lives together and – oh Christ, what am
I doing?

He gets down on one knee.

Well?!

Beat.

Alice (*quietly*)   I can't do this any more.

Beat.

Adrian   What?

Alice   I'm sorry. I didn't want to – I didn't know you were
going to – I just . . . I can't do this any more.

Adrian   Do what?

Alice   Us.

Beat.

Adrian   Are you breaking up with me?

Alice   I'm sorry.

Adrian   You're breaking up with me?!

Alice   I'm sorry.

Adrian   But what – why? – Is this because of before?
Because that was just a stupid fight, Alice, we always fight.
We don't break up over a fight, what are you doing?

Alice   I'm sorry.

Adrian   Stop saying that! If you're sorry, don't do it!

Beat.

I shouldn't have proposed. That was stupid. Forget I said it,
OK? Let's just go to bed, watch a movie . . . 'Cause I just
wanted to apologise, that was all I was trying to do, I got

carried away but I just wanted to say sorry for before, about
the fight, 'cause you were right, you were right, I shouldn't
have got so angry, it was the hormones, I overreacted. I
mean he was dressed as a lion, I was stupid, I . . . I just . . .

Beat.

Are you not even going to tell me why?

Beat.

Alice   I'm gay.

Beat.

Adrian   I've been going too fast. Things have been going
too fast. I know they have, OK? I'm sorry. We can take it
slower. We can take it all slower. Just, give it time and you
can get used to it, you will get used to it.

Alice   I don't want to get used to it.

Beat.

You don't look like her any more. You don't sound like her.
Everything that's her is going. Or gone. And I don't want to
get used to that. I'm gay.

Beat.

Adrian   No you're not.

Alice   What?

Adrian   You're not.

Alice   Yes, I am.

Adrian   No, Alice, you're not. You're not, think about it,
listen to me, how many people have you been with in your
life? Two. Me and Josh. And what's the one thing we've got
in common? We're both men. Don't you see? That's why
you've never come out to your parents, that's why you've
never been able to accept who you are, because it's not who
you are. You fell in love with me, you got confused, but I was

a man the whole time, I was a man and you were straight.
You're not gay. You never have been.

Beat.

Alice   I never have been?

Adrian *shakes his head.*

Pause.

Alice   I was nine years old.

Adrian   What?

Alice   I was nine years old. At a birthday party. At a friend's
house. She had an older sister.

Adrian   What are you talking about?

Alice   I felt butterflies. And I didn't know why at first. I just
looked at her, this girl, she was wearing a leotard, it was
fancy dress, she was a cat, and I just knew that there was
something going on but I didn't know what, and then
suddenly, all at once, it hit me and I realised, 'Oh shit, I like
girls.' And I waited for it to go away, I tried really hard to
make it go away, but it didn't. And even when I went out
with boys, when I went out with Josh, I could never say it but
I knew deep down that I liked girls. I like girls. I like girls,
and I've always liked girls, and I still like girls, and who the
fuck are you to tell me I don't? When I have accepted
everything that you've said to me. You want to be a man? Fine.
You need to change your name? Alright then. You want to
wear those clothes and lift these weights and have an
operation to give yourself a dick? Whatever! I have accepted
that because it was what you wanted, what you needed, who
you are. Fine. And I tried to change, I tried so hard to
change, but there are some things that I can't change, there
are some things I don't want to change because they are part
of who I am. And why is that less important? Why do I just
have to stand aside and deny that because you're going on
your own personal journey? I want you to be happy. I want

you to get what you want. But what you want is to kill the person I love and replace her with someone I don't. Someone I can't. Because I'm gay. You want to be a man? Adrian? You want to be a man? Fine. But I like girls.

Beat.

But how would you know that? You were too busy celebrating the fact that you passed to even notice there was one in our flat.

Pause.

Adrian   That girl . . . ?

Beat.

You . . .

He realises what she's telling him.

Beat.

How long?

Alice   Since New Year. Nothing's happened. But I've wanted it to.

Adrian   So the whole time . . . the whole time I've been . . .

Beat.

'Cause . . . You do know, the way I've kind of got through this, y'know, whenever anyone looked at me funny, or called me names, or laughed at me, or if the hormones made me sick or angry, the way I kind of got through it was just to remember that I had you, and that you understood, or at least you were trying to and that you . . .

Beat.

'Cause if you did have a problem, you know a good time to have mentioned it would have maybe been before I . . .

Beat.

'Cause if you had, maybe I wouldn't have even . . .

Alice   Yes, you would.

Beat.

You would.

Beat.

Adrian (*quietly*)   Alright then, get out.

Alice   What?

Adrian   Go on then, if you're going to go, go. Leave me alone. Get out.

Alice   No, I –

Adrian   *I said get out!*

Beat.

Alice *doesn't move.*

Beat.

Adrian   Alice. I love you.

Beat.

Alice   I loved Fiona. I'm sorry.

She exits.

Adrian *is left on his own.*

Scene Four

De Hoogstraat.

Loud music plays.

Lelani *is dancing, a plastic pint cup in her hand.*

Alice *enters. After a few seconds she sees* **Lelani** *and goes to her.*

Alice (*shouting over the music*)   LANI!

Lelani *turns to see her.*

Lelani   I THOUGHT YOU WEREN'T GOING TO –

Alice *kisses her.*

Lelani   WHAT ABOUT YOUR GIRLFRIEND?

Alice   SHE'S NOT MY GIRLFRIEND ANY MORE! LITERALLY!

She grabs **Lelani**'*s drink.*

Alice   I REALLY NEED THIS!

She downs it and throws the cup away.

Lelani   THERE WERE DRUGS IN THAT!

Alice *laughs.*

Alice   GOOD!

She grabs **Lelani** *and kisses her again.*

Alice   LET'S NOT STOP DOING THIS!

Lelani *takes her by the hand and leads her away.*

Scene Five

Alice *and* **Adrian**'*s flat.*

Josh *is looking at* **Adrian**.

Adrian *is drunk, he has put on one of* **Alice**'*s dresses, it doesn't suit him. Female clothes don't seem to fit any more. His male clothes are scattered around the floor.*

Josh   What happened? Why are you dressed like that? Why have you got that on?

Adrian   She's gone. She's gone, Josh. Said that if I was a man, she couldn't be with me, so . . .

Josh   Oh God . . .

Adrian   I have to go back. I have to go back to how I was.

Josh Adrian –

Adrian I can do it, though, I need to do it. I understand, if one of us needs to change then . . .

Josh Let's get you a drink of water, yeah?

Adrian I asked her to marry me. I asked her to marry me, and then she said that . . . Did you know?

Josh Know what?

Adrian About the girl. The girl from work. Did you know about her?

Josh No.

Beat.

I suspected.

Beat.

Adrian, this isn't going to work.

Adrian No, no, it has to, it has to work.

Josh No. It won't. Look, I know what this feels like. But you can't go back to being something you never were.

Beat.

Adrian It's always been so easy for you, hasn't it?

Josh What?

Adrian Mum and Dad's favourite, did well in school, all the friends, straight, perfect –

Josh Hey, come on now –

Adrian Never had to worry about anything –

Josh Adrian, you're drunk.

Adrian My big brother. Come here to save the day. Telling me what to do.

Josh   No, I wasn't trying to –

Adrian   You understand do you?! You know what it feels like?

Josh   I'm sorry, I didn't mean –

Adrian   You think I'm a man?! You think I'm a man?!

He punches **Josh** *in the face.* **Josh** *stumbles back, surprised.*

Josh   Ow, Jesus –

Adrian   Hit me back!

Josh   What? I'm not going to –

Adrian *hits him again.*

Josh   Ow, fucking hell –

Adrian   Hit me back!

Josh   Adrian –

Adrian *hits him again harder. And again.*

Adrian   Hit me back! Hit me back!

Josh   Stop it –

He tries to push **Adrian** *away,* **Adrian** *keeps trying to hit him even harder.*

Adrian   Hit me back!

Josh   Will you just –

Adrian   Don't push me, hit me! You think I'm a man? Come on then! Hit me! Hit me! HIT ME!

He pounds on **Josh** *with all his strength but* **Josh** *blocks. The punches get weaker as* **Adrian** *breaks down.*

Adrian   Hit me back. Please, just –

He buckles and collapses into **Josh**'s *arms.*

Adrian   Why doesn't she want me? I haven't changed. I haven't . . . I'm still me. Why doesn't she want me? Why doesn't she want me any more?

Josh (*quietly*)   I know. I know.

He holds **Adrian** *as he sobs.*

Scene Six

Lelani's *bedroom.*

Alice *and* **Lelani** *are lying on the bed together.*

They are smoking a joint.

Lelani   Oh my God.

Alice   Yeah.

Lelani   No, I mean. Oh. My. God.

Alice   I know.

Lelani   The whole time?

Alice   Since New Year.

Lelani   Oh my God.

Alice   I know.

Beat.

Lelani   You know you could have told me.

Alice   I didn't know how.

Lelani   I would have understood. Everything makes a lot more sense now.

Alice   I know. I just . . . It was a bit . . . it was a pretty confusing time y'know?

Lelani   I know. But it is OK. You have told me now.

She kisses **Alice**.

Beat.

Lelani   I just don't understand it.

Alice   What?

Lelani   How does it work? With your girlfriend. Does she . . . have a penis? I mean, what does she have down there?

Alice   Erm, nothing. I mean, he still has a, y'know, but it's only been four months.

Lelani   But will she grow one?

Alice   Erm, no, he'd need an operation.

Lelani   What kind of operation?

Alice   I don't know, but he may not even have it, a lot of people don't.

Lelani   They don't?

Alice   No.

Lelani   But what do they have down there?

Alice   Just . . . whatever they have already.

Lelani   Wow.

Beat.

Urgh.

Beat.

Alice   You don't have any Nurofen do you? Y'know, when everything that's just happened just . . . hits you.

Lelani   No. Sorry, I have more wine.

Alice   I think I've had enough.

Lelani   OK.

Beat.

I just find it so weird, y'know? Why would you want to change into a man?

Alice It's not . . . It's more like they're born in the wrong body kind of thing.

Lelani Born in the wrong body?

Alice Yeah. Erm . . . like, he feels like a man, but he had a woman's body – I'm probably not explaining it very well.

Lelani No, I get it, I just . . . surely if you feel like you are in the wrong body there is something maybe wrong up here. Maybe she just needs some therapy.

Alice He.

Lelani What?

Alice It's . . . You just . . . He's a he now.

Lelani Oh. OK.

Beat.

I have had a nice night.

Alice Good.

Lelani I'm glad you decided to come.

Alice Great.

Lelani What are you thinking?

Alice Nothing, really.

Lelani Do you want to know what I'm thinking? I'm thinking that I always knew I wanted to come to Rotterdam, but I never knew why. Until now.

Beat.

Alice *gets up.*

Alice Right. Y'know what, I might actually just head.

Lelani Why?

Alice   Well, Wouter'll be back soon.

Lelani   He won't be back for hours.

Alice   Yeah, but I think I just need to collect my thoughts.

Lelani   You can do that here.

Alice *picks up* **Lelani***'s laptop and opens it.*

Alice   I'd really rather just – Is it alright if I use this? I just want to find the nearest hotel, I . . .

She looks at the screen.

Beat.

Why are you logged into my email?

Lelani   It was a surprise. I was going to tell you in the morning.

Alice   Tell me what?

Lelani   I really like you Alice, I just want you to be able to be honest about who you are.

Alice   I don't understand.

Lelani   Now, you might be shocked, but I really think it is better now.

Alice   I don't know what you're talking about. Did you log in? How do you know my password?

Lelani   You gave it to me. When your phone was broken. It's your name.

Alice   Yeah, but – Lelani, why are you in my email?

Lelani   Well, I knew you wrote to your parents, but never sent it.

Alice   What?

Lelani   So I searched in your drafts, when you were in the bathroom –

Alice No.

Lelani And I cut some stuff out.

Alice You didn't.

Lelani And then I sent it.

Beat.

Alice *laughs.*

Alice It's a joke. Right? You're joking.

Lelani No.

Alice *stops laughing.*

Alice No. You *are* joking.

Lelani No. I'm not.

Alice This isn't funny.

Lelani I'm not joking.

Beat.

Alice Sorry, you . . . I mean, I . . . I . . . I mean you – what have you . . . ? What the fuck have you done? Why did you – ? What were you thinking?

Lelani No, listen, I am trying to help you.

Alice Help me? Help me? What about this do you think is helpful?!

Lelani It's what you wanted.

Alice What I wanted? You think I wanted you to out me to my parents?

Lelani I didn't, you wrote the email to them, I just gave it a push.

Alice A push? You think that was a push? That was not a push! A push would have been – I don't know what a push would have been but this was not a fucking push!

She bends over, hyperventilating.

I've got to get out of here.

Lelani   Are you OK? You're breathing funny.

Alice   I know I am, I'm hyperventilating.

Lelani   Do you want a paper bag?

Alice   No, I don't want a paper bag! I want you to have not sent that fucking email!

Lelani   But it's OK, don't you see? Now we can be together.

Alice   What?

Lelani   Now we can be together. Alice, I . . . I love you.

Alice   What?

Lelani   I want to be with you.

Alice   You want to be with me?

Lelani   And you want to be with me too, no?

Alice   What? No.

Lelani   No?

Alice   No.

Lelani   But I thought – that's why you're here, that's why you left your girlfriend.

Alice   What?

Lelani   You left your girlfriend to be with me.

Alice   No, I didn't, I didn't leave her because of you, I left her because of her. Because of him. Him. He's not a her, he's a him, he's not my girlfriend, he's my boyfriend. He's a man, OK?

Lelani   I don't understand.

Alice   He's a man! He's always been a man. I don't care if he hasn't got a penis, he doesn't need therapy – he's a man!

Lelani   No, I mean I don't understand, I thought this is what you wanted. I thought you wanted to stay with me here in Rotterdam.

Alice   I never wanted to stay in Rotterdam.

Lelani   But you said you did.

Alice   No, I didn't.

Lelani   You did, you did!

Alice   No I didn't. I never said I wanted to stay. I just . . . didn't say I didn't. I wasn't declaring my undying love. I was just . . .

Beat.

I was being polite.

Scene Seven

Alice *and* **Adrian**'s *flat.*

Adrian's *clothes are still scattered everywhere.*

Josh *is packing them up,* **Alice** *is desperate.*

Alice   Gone? What do you mean gone? He can't be gone? Where would he go?

Josh   I don't know, Alice, I didn't ask. But he went about an hour ago. Took some stuff and left.

Alice   But why?

Josh   Why do you think?

Beat.

Alice   And you're going too?

Josh   Tomorrow.

Alice   Tomorrow?

Josh   Yeah. I think I've put it off long enough.

Alice   Yeah, but tomorrow, I mean, can't you wait a few days? I could really use your help right now.

Josh   They're your parents, Alice. Not mine.

Alice   Yeah, but I can't talk to them, Josh, not on my own. Please, you've got to stay.

Josh   I've got to stay?

Alice   Yes, please, Josh, it's me, I'm asking you.

Josh   And I'm telling you I'm going.

Beat.

Alice   Then let me come too.

Josh   What?

Alice   I'll . . . I'll come with you. Wherever you're going . . . I'll come too. I mean, I can't go home, I don't want to stay here, so why not? Let's go, travel, find somewhere different, somewhere away from all of this, you and me, Josh . . . please.

Pause.

Josh   Alice, you're a coward.

Alice   What?

Josh   It's OK, I am too. I should have told him months ago what was going to happen. I wanted to. The whole time I wanted to say, 'Watch out, I've been where you are and I know how this ends, but I just couldn't bring myself to say it. It was like watching a bad remake of a film you didn't like the first time round. Oh, it's that scene, is it?

Alice   I . . . I didn't mean for this to happen.

Josh   No, no, of course you didn't mean for it to happen, you never mean for it to happen.

Beat.

Do you remember why you first came here?

Alice   The job.

Josh   Yeah, but there were others you could have taken.

Alice   No, it was the best.

Josh   No, it wasn't.

Alice   Well, it was the most interesting.

Josh   Nope. It was here. That's why you chose it. Because you didn't think I'd come too.

Alice   That's not true –

Josh   Yes, it is. You've spent the last seven years in Rotterdam – somewhere you didn't want to be in the first place – because you were too scared to tell me the truth. That you didn't want to be with me. And you know what the worst part is? I've spent seven years here too. Most people would have gone when their girlfriend left them for their sister, not me. I soldiered on. And as a reward I got to watch it happen all over again. Except this time it's worse, you know why? 'Cause I only realised what was missing with us when I first saw you with her. Him. I didn't realise that you never really loved me until I saw you with him. The thing is, Alice, if you ask me to stay, if you ask me that, if you ask to come with me, if you ask me anything . . . I'll probably say yes. I'll always say yes to you. So, I guess, what I'm saying is . . . Please don't ask me to. If that's alright.

He closes his bag and exits.

Scene Eight

The Rotterdam–Hull ferry departure lounge.

Adrian *sits, a bag by his side, waiting.*

Announcer (*voice-over*)   *Dames en heren, de veerboot naar Hull van twaalf uur zal over vijftien minuten beginnen met boarden.*

Beat.

(*Voice-over.*) Ladies and gentlemen, the twelve o'clock ferry to Hull will begin boarding in fifteen minutes.

A long pause.

In **Alice** *and* **Adrian**'s *flat.* **Lelani** *enters,* **Josh** *follows.*

Lelani   Is Alice here?

Josh   Hey, wait, you can't –

Lelani   I need to see her.

Josh   Hey –

Lelani   Alice!

Josh   She won't want to see you, I know who you are, I know what happened.

Lelani   Oh yeah? She told you? She told you what she did? The *stomme kankerwijf*! My boss comes home and finds me crying and asks me why so I tell him and then he loses his shit and starts shouting like an asshole because he's in love with me or something and I slept with someone from work and so I said 'Fuck you!' and I left and now I have no job and nowhere to live and it's all because of that *verdomde kut hoer*!

Josh   Hey, look, this isn't the time –

Lelani *charges past him.*

Josh   Hey, you can't just – that's not her room, that's mine –

Lelani *charges back in and then out again.*

Josh *notices a letter.*

He picks it up and reads.

Lelani (*off*)   Alice?! Alice, where are you?! Alice?! Alice!

She re-enters.

She's not here! Where is she?!

Josh   Gone.

He shows her the letter.

She's gone.

In the departure lounge, **Alice** *enters, carrying a large bag.*

She walks to where **Adrian** *is sitting and sits a few seats away from him.*

He doesn't acknowledge her.

They sit in silence.

Josh   Are you OK?

Lelani   Duh! Yes! I'm fine. I don't care about her! That stupid fucking Engels bitch can go the fuck to hell!

Josh   Well, you sound like you're taking it well.

Lelani *tries to hold back tears.*

Josh   Look, it probably hurts quite a lot right now, but . . . it'll be OK. The best thing you can do when you've had your heart broken is just try not to get hooked up on it, y'know, let yourself move on.

Lelani   Duh. You think I care about her? I am twenty-one years old. There are lots of people out there who would want to be with me.

Josh   Oh. Well, yeah, absolutely.

Beat.

And, look, if you've seriously got nowhere to go, you could always crash here for a few nights.

Lelani   What? I am not staying here. This city is shit. I hate it. I wish I had never come here. I am going to go and live in Amsterdam.

She goes to leave, then stops.

None of this was personal.

Josh   None of what?

Lelani   Anything. You look very convincing by the way. If I hadn't known, I wouldn't have guessed. Shame about the hands.

She leaves.

Beat.

He realises what she meant.

Josh   Hey wait, no, I'm not – No! No, I'm . . .

He gives up.

Beat.

He looks at the note one last time, scrunches it up, and throws it away.

He exits.

Silence.

Alice   You bought the tickets on my computer.

Beat.

That's how I knew you were here . . .

Beat.

I'm not here to stop you, I mean – I don't want to . . . I shouldn't have come, I'm sorry.

Beat.

My parents know. About me. And I slept with that girl. I should say that right up front. I mean, it was a mistake, and I know that's not an excuse but . . . No, it is an excuse, people only say that's not an excuse when they're trying to give an excuse.

Beat.

She . . . sent that email . . . to my parents. Kind of a weird thing to do. But . . . she did it.

Beat.

Still, at least I win the bet.

Silence.

Y'know, I've been really angry at you. For a long time now. I've actually really hated you. 'Cause, when you first told me . . . It was like I was just expected to be OK with it. Like I should feel guilty if I didn't just go, 'Oh yeah, sure, fine, do whatever you want.' Because I wasn't OK. I wasn't OK with it. But I wasn't allowed to say that. I wasn't allowed to say anything because the person I used to talk to about stuff like that was my girlfriend. And she was changing. She was changing and I wasn't allowed to tell her that that wasn't OK. I wasn't allowed to tell her that I didn't want her to change. And that made me pretty fucking angry actually. So yeah, I really hated you for that.

Beat.

But actually . . . I think it might have been easier if you'd just . . . changed more. 'Cause I think I was prepared for that. If you'd just become a completely different person I think I could have just walked away and – I dunno, mourned and moved on, but . . . 'Cause I used to picture us getting older, y'know, with kids and a mortgage, old women in a care home, still bickering and disagreeing and going to bed together every night. I used to think about which of us would die first and how I'd cope if it was . . . So when you told me that . . . I think it would have been easier if you'd just changed more. 'Cause then I could have just said goodbye and moved on.

Beat.

But then last night, when I was . . . kissing her . . . Every time I opened my eyes it was just . . . the wrong face. And I just kept thinking about the person who should have been there. But when I did I wasn't thinking 'I want Fee' or 'I want Adrian'. It was just . . . I want you.

Beat.

And I know I got it wrong. I fucked up. I know that now but I'm here. At the very least, y'know? I'm here now.

Silence.

Adrian   You don't win.

Alice   What?

Adrian   The bet.

Beat.

I said you wouldn't come out before Angelina Jolie. You don't win if someone did it for you.

Beat.

Alice   OK.

Pause.

Adrian   How did you get through the gate?

Alice   Bought a ticket.

Adrian   Are you coming?

Alice   Do you want me to?

Adrian   Don't you want to stay?

Alice   Not enough.

Adrian   What about your work?

Alice   Er . . . Fuck work?

Beat.

I mean, I'll probably try and take compassionate leave, I might have to come back and work out my notice, but for the time being . . . I have pretty much everything I need in this bag, so . . .

Adrian   I'm going to stay with my parents.

Alice   OK.

Adrian   I want to talk to them properly . . . about this.

Alice   Me too. I mean I want to talk to mine.

Beat.

But I could . . . I mean, if you wanted . . .

Beat.

I found this. In the flat.

She takes the binder out of her bag and puts it down on the seat between them.

You don't have to do this on your own.

She holds out her hand.

Adrian *looks at it.*

Silence.

He grasps her hand.

They both look away again, but neither lets go.

Adrian   So . . . what happens now?

Alice   I don't know.

Beat.

Adrian   Well, don't worry. Neither do I.

They keep hold of each other's hands.

'Rotterdam' by The Beautiful South plays.

The scene fades away.

*But **Adrian** and **Alice** don't let go.*

The End.

Bloomsbury Methuen Drama Modern Plays

include work by

Bola Agbaje
Edward Albee
Davey Anderson
Jean Anouilh
John Arden
Peter Barnes
Sebastian Barry
Alistair Beaton
Brendan Behan
Edward Bond
William Boyd
Bertolt Brecht
Howard Brenton
Amelia Bullmore
Anthony Burgess
Leo Butler
Jim Cartwright
Lolita Chakrabarti
Caryl Churchill
Lucinda Coxon
Curious Directive
Nick Darke
Shelagh Delaney
Ishy Din
Claire Dowie
David Edgar
David Eldridge
Dario Fo
Michael Frayn
John Godber
Paul Godfrey
James Graham
David Greig
John Guare
Mark Haddon
Peter Handke
David Harrower
Jonathan Harvey
Iain Heggie

Robert Holman
Caroline Horton
Terry Johnson
Sarah Kane
Barrie Keeffe
Doug Lucie
Anders Lustgarten
David Mamet
Patrick Marber
Martin McDonagh
Arthur Miller
D. C. Moore
Tom Murphy
Phyllis Nagy
Anthony Neilson
Peter Nichols
Joe Orton
Joe Penhall
Luigi Pirandello
Stephen Poliakoff
Lucy Prebble
Peter Quilter
Mark Ravenhill
Philip Ridley
Willy Russell
Jean-Paul Sartre
Sam Shepard
Martin Sherman
Wole Soyinka
Simon Stephens
Peter Straughan
Kate Tempest
Theatre Workshop
Judy Upton
Timberlake Wertenbaker
Roy Williams
Snoo Wilson
Frances Ya-Chu Cowhig
Benjamin Zephaniah

For a complete listing of Bloomsbury
Methuen Drama titles, visit:
www.bloomsbury.com/drama

Follow us on Twitter and keep up to date
with our news and publications
@MethuenDrama